GUIDE
TO
SPIRITUAL HEALING

GUIDE
TO
SPIRITUAL HEALING

David Geddes

CAXTON REFERENCE

© 2000 Caxton Editions

This edition published 2000 by Caxton Editions,
20 Bloomsbury Street, London, WC1B 3QA.

Caxton Editions is an imprint of the Caxton Publishing Group.

Printed and bound in India.

CONTENTS

INTRODUCTION

At the beginning of this new century it is natural
to look ahead and ponder the changes and
scientific advances which lie ahead. It is also
sobering to consider the huge strides made in
science and technology in the mere 100 years of
the twentieth century. Powered flight was born
in the early years of the century and now
commercial flight to all parts of the globe is
commonplace. We now have radio, television
and computers. Man has walked on the moon
and satellites in space circle the world providing
communications and information on a myriad
of subjects. Medicine has wiped out many of the
killing diseases and illnesses that have plagued
mankind, although new dangerous diseases are
now appearing. For a time it seemed that science
was all-powerful and all conquering, but in

recent years there has been a feeling of disillusionment with man's own efforts, especially in the face of new killer diseases and a growing number of natural disasters. More and more people in the developed world are searching for a deeper meaning for their lives and many are turning to spirituality, which can be found in many forms. Although interest in organised religion seems to be waning, there is a growing interest in the meaning of existence and spiritual considerations that cannot be explained by science alone.

There is now recognition that diet, lifestyle and exercise are important factors in a healthy life and there is also a growing awareness that emotional and spiritual wellbeing have beneficial effects on general health. Traditional medicine now acknowledges the worth of alternative medicine and homeopathy in the treatment of disease and often combines with them to produce a holistic approach.

Many of the alternative therapies have been practised for many centuries but were suppressed during the advance of what we know as traditional medicine. For a long time people dealing in the paranormal or psychic area were treated with suspicion or even derision, but in recent years there has been a growing consciousness and interest in all levels of experience and people are realising that a scientific answer cannot always be provided for every problem.

In this new climate the interest in healing is expanding and so is the number of people calling themselves healers. The terms used are usually 'faith healing' or 'spiritual healing'. Faith healing has had a fairly bad press in recent years, especially in the United States, the land of fraudulent television evangelists and healers. It has also been found to be a restrictive term as it implies that a religious faith has to be held before healing can take place. This is not the case. We will, however, deal with the place of healing in the Christian message in this book. Spiritual healing is a term which is much more widely acceptable as it covers all people, whether holding a religious faith or not. The rise in the number of healers indicates that the power to heal lies within many of us and the ability to transfer energy through touching is much more normal than is generally believed.

There is a growing realisation that many diseases, if not all, come from the mind or are related to stress. It is now recognised that all suppressed emotions, stress and over-work can be the cause of many medical conditions. Because faith or spiritual healing cannot always stand up to scientific investigations and explanation, it can easily be denigrated. Thankfully, many more minds are being opened to the possibilities and successes of this type of healing and it is admitted that present orthodox medical knowledge is not perfect. More and more, it is the case that spiritual healing is taking its place as a complementary therapy to be used side by side with orthodox medicine and that it is not intended as a replacement.

Chapter 1
HEALING AND CHRISTIANITY

The ministry of Jesus Christ lasted only three years and took place in a small area on the fringe of the Roman Empire. The effect of this ministry has, however, changed the world and shaped the civilisations of large parts of the world. An important factor in gaining the attention of the people and the spreading of his message was his ministry of healing. This is clearly shown in St Luke's Gospel chapter 5 from verse 17, using the William Barclay translation:

One day, as Jesus was teaching, a group of Pharisees and legal experts were sitting listening. They had come from every village in Galilee and from Judaea and from Jerusalem. The Lord's power made Jesus able to make sick people well. A party of men came carrying on a bed a man who was paralysed. They tried to carry him in to lay him in front of Jesus. They were unable to find any way to carry him in because of the crowd. So they went up on to the roof, and they let him down, bed and all, through the tiles, right into the middle of the crowd, in front of Jesus. When Jesus saw their faith he said: 'Man, your sins are forgiven you'. Then questions began to arise in the minds of the experts in the Law and of the Pharisees. 'Who is this fellow who is insulting God?' they said. 'Can anyone but God forgive sins?' Jesus was well aware of what was going on in their minds. 'What are your minds going on about?' he said. 'Which is easier, to say, "Your sins are forgiven", or to say, "Get up and walk?" Just to show you that the Son of Man actually has power to forgive sins on earth' – he said to the paralysed man– 'Get up I tell you! Lift your bedding and go home!' On the spot the man got up in front of them all, lifted the mattress on which he had been lying, and went away home, praising God. They were absolutely astonished. They kept on praising God; they were filled with awe. 'We have seen things beyond belief today', they said.

Jesus made a statement of his position and message by the use of healing. He also silenced the religious and legal arguments being brought against him.

Throughout the ministry of Jesus his compassion reached out to the ordinary people with healing. In Mark chapter 3 we are told that Jesus with his disciples, withdrew to the lakeside in Galilee and the crowds flocked to him:

The crowd was so dense that he told his disciples to keep a boat ready to avoid being crushed by the crowd, for he performed many cures, and the result was that all who were suffering from the scourges of disease rushed forward to touch him. Whenever the unclean spirits saw him, they flung themselves down at his feet. 'You are the Son of God' they kept shouting. But he strictly ordered them not to surround him with publicity.

Jesus constantly equated healing with sin and the whole person-a technique not dissimilar to the modern day idea of holistic healing. He used touch in his healing and sometimes spittle, which was a recognised method at that time. He appeared to have an aura of healing surrounding him and people would touch his robe, looking for healing. In Mark chapter 5 we hear of a young woman suffering from a haemorrhage who has spent her last penny trying to find a cure:

She had heard the stories about Jesus. She came up behind him in the crowd and touched his cloak, for she said to herself: 'If I touch even his clothes, I will be cured.' There and then her flow of blood was staunched and she felt in her body that she was cured of the trouble that had been her scourge for so long. Jesus was aware that his power had gone out of him. Immediately he swung round in the crowd. 'Who touched my clothes?' he said. The disciples said to him 'Don't you see the crowd jostling you on every side? What's the sense in asking who touched you?' But Jesus continued to search the crowd with his eyes to discover who had done it. The woman was so scared that she was still shaking. She knew what had happened to her. So she came and threw herself at Jesus feet and told him the whole truth. 'Daughter,' he said, 'your faith has cured you. Go and God bless you! Go and enjoy your new health, free from the trouble that was your scourge!'

The healings of Jesus have often been

questioned but it is very clear that they were an essential part of his life and of his ministry. They revealed him as compassionate and aware of the problems of the people around him. The people of Israel in Jesus' day understood the holistic view of the whole person-body and soul. These had to be harmonised within the healing process. Holism is therefore shown not to be a new philosophy, but one that has its basis in many older traditions.

After the crucifixion of Jesus, the disciples, and then the apostles, did his bidding and went out to spread the good news and heal. Healing was very important in the early church and in many ways helped to establish Christianity in the face of many other sects. Many cures were carried out by Peter, Paul and Jerome and all of the disciples and apostles contributed to the healing which became an integral part of the activities of the early church. With the demise of the apostles, the importance of healing began to wane in the church. As the church became more powerful in the Middle Ages, it turned against the healing tradition which it considered pagan, and eventually almost all healing was banned in Europe. This led to a separation of religion and medicine, the soul and the body, and the holistic approach of Jesus' healing ministry was lost. Down through the following years, many thinkers and philosophers attacked the Christian ideas of healing and miracles, among them Descartes, Spinoza and Thomas Hobbes. This lead to the essay in 1748 by David Hume which said that miracles were a violation of the laws of nature. In modern times there have been many suggestions by scholars and theologians that the healings and miracles performed by Jesus should not be taken literally and that they were merely symbolic.

In many branches of the church today, especially in the newer evangelical congregations, the tradition of healing is being revived. Even in the more traditional churches healing services are becoming more common. It is to be hoped that this ministry which was fundamental to the young christian church will return to its central position. For too long the church has placed too much emphasis on the significance of suffering in the development of faith and not enough on the positive aspect of healing. Even St Augustine who, in his earlier years railed against healing, eventually realised his error and said, 'I realised how many miracles were occurring in our own day and which were so like the miracles of old-how wrong it would be to allow the memory of these marvels of divine power to perish from among our people.'

Perhaps the movement within the church towards greater emphasis on healing will return the ministry to the centre of the faith. In Matthew chapter 15 we read:

Jesus left there and went along the coast of the lake of Galilee. He climbed the hill and sat there and the crowds flocked to him bringing those who were lame and blind, crippled and deaf, and suffering from many other diseases. They laid them at his feet and he cured them. His power to heal left the crowd amazed when they saw the dumb speaking, the crippled restored to fitness, the lame walking, and the blind seeing, and they praised the God of Israel.

CHAPTER 2

HEALING IN HISTORY

The history of healing stretches back to the beginning of recorded time. Faith healing or spiritual healing has been integral to all cultures and religions. All primitive peoples have had their medicine man and these are still evident in vast areas of Africa and Asia. The Ancient Greeks and Romans had temples to Asclepius, the god of medicine, and the Old Testament has numerous instances of healing, going back to the days of distant history.

There are many branches of what is considered unorthodox healing covering the treatment of all types of diseases. These are variously called faith healing, spiritual healing, fringe medicine, or sometimes miracle cures. This whole area has often laid itself open to charges of superstition and trickery – and there has been much of both over the years. From the itinerant sellers of quack bottles of medicine to cure all ills, to characters like James Graham of Edinburgh who sold beds to provide painless childbirth, chairs to remedy rheumatism and elixirs of life.

We have already seen that spiritual healing is as old as man himself. The popularity of healing has gone in cycles and was especially strong about 500 years before Christ. There was great emphasis then on the importance of rest, diet and fresh air in the war against disease, but gradually the use of drugs gained ground and became part of the healing process. With the advent of Christianity, the drug cures declined and there was a return to pure faith or spiritual healing. This maintained its pre-eminent position for many hundreds of years before it was overtaken again by more orthodox medicine. It might be interesting to consider some of the significant personalities who have emerged from the long story of healing.

Gnosticism

As the early Christian Church was establishing itself in the 2nd and 3rd centuries, another movement came into being which appeared to have many similarities with Christianity and therefore could have detracted from the impact of the still new religion. The movement was called Gnosticism, the name being derived from the Greek word 'gnosis', meaning 'knowledge'. The Gnostics believed that they were in possession of a special knowledge which came from divine revelation and was available to only a chosen few. They believed that Jesus was the primary source of this revelation.

This new philosophy had many of the attributes of a religion and it became fairly popular, although it was made up of a wide range of doctrines and ideas. There are many branches and schools of thought within the movement but the basic belief is that there is a divine presence within man which can be activated by means of revelation. In the 2nd century Valentinus was a leading teacher in the Gnostic movement and he taught that human beings fall into three types: spiritual, psychic and fleshly.

The spiritual beings are those open to divine revelation – the Gnostics.

The psychic beings have a soul, and by using their free will can aspire to moving upwards and becoming spiritual – the Christians.

The fleshly beings are those who do not aspire to higher things and sink into materialism and things of the flesh. They can have no hope of true knowledge and salvation.

Valentinus claimed that his theories of the three classes of human beings were based on the teachings and sayings of Jesus and St. Paul in the New Testament.

The Gnostics believe that the world was not created by God and is, therefore, evil. They think that the God of Gods could not have created anything that was not completely perfect and that the only possibility of salvation for man is by rising from the material into the spiritual. They believe that the material body is evil, in contrast to the spirit, which can be divine. They consider that Jesus assumed his Christ-like qualities during his lifetime and at his crucifixion he did not die, but ascended to God from whom he came.

The background of Gnosticism has not really been discovered, but it is thought that it originated in the Middle East and Greece from various philosophical and religious strands. It is thought that some of the ideas came from Plato, the Greek philosopher. Little was known about the movement in present times until a large number of Gnostic texts were discovered during diggings being carried out in Egypt in 1945. The texts were translated into English and published as *The Nag Hammadi Library* in 1977.

Asclepius

It is not known whether Asclepius was a real figure in history or mythical. In the first half of the fourth century BC Archias received on injury while hunting and was suitably cured by treatment given to him by Asclepius. He was so deeply affected by his experience that he founded a temple to Asclepius at Pergamon.

Asclepius had already been recognised as a healer of diseases and the Asclepeion at Pergamon is perhaps the most famous medical site of the Greco-Roman era and is well preserved. The cult of Asclepius produced a cure requiring the patient to spend a night in an incubation temple, believing that the gods would effect a cure in a dream. The patient was purified and his dreams were interpreted by the priests, with a view to formulating care and treatment for the ailment. There were many stories of the cures that were brought about at Pergamon relating to lamers, infertility and psychologically induced illnesses. The Greek developments in medicine were also embraced by the Romans, who first produced a public hospital system.

Pythagoras

This was the Greek mathematician who discovered the geometrical theorem named after him. He was a philosopher and religious leader and the members of his religious society followed an ascetic regime of dietary taboos, self-examination and study. He held healing in high regard and considered it an important part of his ideas on philosophy. His followers believed that matter is composed of opposites in conflict and that they have to be in equilibrium in order to produce harmony.

Hippocrates

Although he was not the first to establish a medical practice, Hippocrates is generally reckoned to be the father of modern medicine. He founded the Hippocratic School of medicine which greatly influenced medical science until the 18th century. His followers believed that health depended on the balance of four body fluids, or humours: phlegm, blood, black bile and yellow bile. Hippocrates lived from 460–377 BC and was born on the Greek island of Kos. He received his general and also his initial medical education on Kos before moving to Athens where he gained great expertise in the diagnosis, prognosis and treatment of many diseases, including tuberculosis, hysteria and epilepsy. He also dealt with arthritis and argued that all diseases were caused by organic injury or the imbalance of bodily fluids, which we have already mentioned.

He believed that the body had self-healing powers and that the doctor could aid these natural processes. We have already mentioned the importance given to rest, diet and fresh air by the medical fraternity at the time of Hippocrates and he also recognised the healing properties of the laying on of hands. He had his own ideas on healing energy and believed that the flow of this energy could be distributed by non-benign forces which upset the balance of the body. He suggested that mind and body were separate and this idea was accepted for many hundreds of years.

Valentine Greatrakes

This important British healer was born in 1628 and was a cavalry officer in the Roundhead army during the Civil War. He became convinced that he had been ordained by God to cure disease. When he first announced the belief in his calling, he was treated with great scepticism and even his wife stated that his powers of healing were solely the result of idle imagination. He did, however, go ahead to test his powers of healing with considerable success. He became known as the Stroker, because of the way he moved his hands as if stroking, although he did not touch his patient's body. He was a rich man with an estate in Ireland and he took no money for his healing services. Greatrakes became a famous figure and he was feted when he visited London in 1666. He then appeared to have fewer and fewer successes and he returned to the quieter life of his estate in Ireland.

The King's Evil

This was the name given to the disease scrofula, which is an ulceration of a lymph node infected with tuberculosis, most commonly in the neck. It was formerly known as king's evil because of the belief that it could be cured by the touch of the sovereign. For many centuries the touch of the king was considered to have healing properties and this became more and more popular during the reigns of the Tudors and the Stuarts. The king would pray, touch the sufferer and give him a coin. The coin was originally silver and then was replaced by gold. By the time of Charles I the healing powers were believed to reside in the coins. In the reign of Charles II, 5,000 sufferers a year were touched by the king.

Franz Mesmer

This was an Austrian physician who claimed to cure diseases by correcting the flow of 'animal magnetism' in his patients' bodies during séance group sessions. The term 'mesmerism' was applied to his practice of waving his hands over his patients' faces and gazing deeply into their eyes. As a fully qualified doctor, Mesmer wished to gain acceptance from the medical profession for his powers and in 1784 in France a commission investigated mesmerism and concluded that any cures were due to the powers of suggestion. Mesmer's claims stimulated serious study of hypnosis by such men as James Braid.

Grigori Rasputin

A Russian mystic, who was a favourite of Tsar Nicholas II and especially Tsarina Alexandra. A Siberian peasant, Rasputin's apparent ability to ease the bleeding of the haemophilic crown prince brought him considerable influence over the royal family. He had travelled through Russia performing cures and tales of his healing powers grew until he came to the attention of the royal family. He had also gained notoriety as a womaniser and this brought him unpopularity and hatred among the courtiers and people of influence. His wild sexuality scandalised St Petersburg and stories circulated about him and the Tsarina. This led to his murder by a group of nobles. His assassins attempted to poison him and when this inexplicably failed he was shot and thrown into the River Neva.

Felix Kersten

Kersten was born in Finland but spent much of his early life in Holland. Beginning with massage, he moved on to a broader interest in various illnesses and discovered that by the laying on of hands he could diagnose ailments. In common with many healers, he found that he felt energy flowing from his hands to the body of the patient when he laid his hands on them. He developed a real ability to relieve pain and his reputation grew, as did his practice. He became a personal doctor to the Dutch royal family and in 1938 he was asked to help Heinreich Himmler, head of the Nazi SS. Himmler suffered from severe stomach problems and orthodox medicine was giving no relief. It is said that Kersten was able to banish the pains at an initial session of only 5 minutes and he so impressed Himmler that he became his personal doctor. In addition to the healing, which he brought to Himmler, he tried to use his influence with this evil man to aid the Jewish peoples. It is thought that he was instrumental in persuading the head of the SS to cancel action against the Jews of Finland and to release numbers of prisoners in concentration camps to Sweden.

Jose de Freitas

The story of de Freitas, known as Arigo to his followers, is a strange one indeed. His first known venture into the world of medicine was very dramatic. He was at the bedside of the dying wife of a friend when he reached for a kitchen knife, and, without warning, cut into her stomach and extracted a large tumour. Afterwards Arigo had no memory of what he had done. The patient made a full recovery and stated that she felt no pain during this unexpected operation. The amazing fact is that Arigo was an uneducated miner and had no medical training whatsoever. Jose de Freitas was a sensation in Brazil during the 1950's and his methods were often insanitary and unorthodox including, at times, the use of kitchen knives, scissors and whatever was at hand.

Although he was jailed twice by the

authorities in Brazil, his fame spread and pilgrimages were made to his home by the sick looking for cures. In 1968 he treated over 1000 people while being watched by a team of doctors. Almost all of the diagnosis which he made were correct and the team of doctors was very impressed. He was killed in a car crash after informing his friends that they would not see him again.

Djuna Davitashvili

This is the best known healer in Russia and her own clinic in Moscow is flourishing. Davitashvili was a qualified medical researcher before embarking on her own brand of spiritual healing. She claims to use bioenergy in partnership with massage and she has achieved an impressive success rate. She comes from the south of the former Soviet Union and she ministered to Leonid Breshnev. It is said that the recently retired president of Russia, Boris Yeltsin has also consulted her. Djuna Davitashvili has long been known for her success with diagnosis and she took part in tests for the Washington Research Centre, in which she diagnosed a group of 43 patients with an accuracy of 97 percent. It is hardly surprising that a prominent healer should emerge from a country that has strong connections with folk medicine and belief in such healing.

Part of the present day renewal of interest in spiritual healing comes from the emergence of the New Age movement, which believes that a worldwide spiritual awakening will come as we enter the Age of Aquarius. We have shown that throughout history spiritual healing has often been repressed but has risen again to aid what is known as orthodox medicine. New Age healing takes a more psychological approach to healing and uses many of the ideas of Freud in the importance of childhood traumas and upsets. They think that experiences of the past must be faced and understood before healing can be successful.

This chapter has looked at some of the aspects of spiritual healing in history and also some of the notable exponents down through the ages. There appears now to be a greater willingness to take healing more seriously and for it to be used in conjunction with orthodox medicine.

Chapter 3
MIRACLE HEALING

This book is dealing with all aspects of spiritual healing and touches on other complementary therapies that either overlap with healing or are in some way related. It is, however, useful to consider another facet of healing which also stretches back thousands of years and is still with us today – miracle healing. Miracle healing is almost invariably focussed on some special or holy site to which people come with high hopes of a cure for some illnesses or disease. Whether the belief and expectation which draws the sick person to the site is instrumental in bringing about a cure or alleviation is impossible to say. The fame of such places is spread by word of mouth and accounts of unexplained cures spread quickly. The ill and the lame are often brought great distances by their family or friends and the experience is highly emotional and, in some instances, spiritual. Such quests for miracle healing has taken place and still takes place in all parts of the world under the aegis of various religions and creeds. Whether it be a temple, the village where a revered guru lives or a church with some special status, the motivation of the pilgrims is the same – a desperate hope of a miracle cure.

In a recent television programme, an investigation was carried out on ancient graves that were discovered in the tiny village of Wing in Buckinghamshire. The graves were beside the church and one, which intrigued the archaeologists, was that of a child of about 12 years of age. From studying the teeth they were convinced that the child had suffered various illnesses and after DNA testing they established that this was the body of a girl of about 12 years old. She was a Saxon who died around 800 to 900 AD. The television investigators sought the help of local children in finding out more about the history of the village and, among other things, they discovered that the church was originally built in Saxon times and dated from about 700 AD. One part of the church, including the crypt, was part of the original building. The fascinating fact then emerged that over 1,000 years ago the crypt had contained some christian relics, including what was believed to be a piece of the holy cross. This information was the final piece of proof required to perhaps suggest the answer to the question of why this sick girl had been buried in that particular place over a thousand years ago. The relics in the church would have made this a place of pilgrimage and it is perfectly reasonable to deduce that the girl's parents had brought her to the church in the hope of a healing at that holy place. Churches throughout christendom held relics of saints and martyrs and were visited by pilgrims and people seeking healing.

There are many places of christian pilgrimage throughout Europe and one with an interesting story is Santiago de Compostela in Galicia in north west Spain. The legend is that St James, possibly the brother of Jesus, travelled as a missionary to Spain and lived for a time in this remote corner of the country. He eventually returned to Jerusalem and was executed in 62 AD. Knowing of his love for Spain, his friends took his body back there and buried him in what became Santiago de Compostela. In the Middle Ages Santiago became a place of pilgrimage and many thousands still make the journey there every year. Among the more famous places of pilgrimage are Fatima in Portugal and Knock in the Republic of Ireland. Knock became a place of pilgrimage after visions of the Virgin Mary were allegedly seen there in 1879. The village now has its own airport, a new church was opened in 1976 and Pope John Paul II visited Knock in 1979. It is obvious that the days of pilgrimage are not over.

By far the most famous and most visited place of pilgrimage is Lourdes in south west France at the foot of the Pyrenees. It was here in 1858 that a local peasant girl called Bernadette claimed that she saw an apparition of the Virgin Mary. In all she claimed that the vision appeared to her eighteen times at a grotto near the village. The girl was only fourteen years old and her parish priest and many people from the village and surrounding area did not believe her. The stories of the visions spread and the belief grew that miracle cures could be received for all types of illnesses by drinking the water from a spring which Bernadette had found in the grotto. More and more people poured into the village to the annoyance of many and still the priest did not believe her, going as far as to call her a liar. Eventually he witnessed a scene when molten wax from a candle fell on Bernadette's hands without causing her pain or scarring the hands. This so-called miracle seems to have banished the remaining doubts about the visions and pilgrims began arriving in the village from all parts of the world. Normal life was no longer open to Bernadette and she became a nun at the age of 20 and died aged 35. She was canonised in 1933.

Huge numbers of people visit Lourdes each year although many of them are tourists drawn by the reputation and stories about the place. It is, however, true that countless numbers have made the pilgrimage since Bernadette had her visions in 1858 and thousands of these have claimed that they have been cured of whichever disease was afflicting them. It is, however, impossible to know how many cures are indeed that, or results brought about by fervour and perhaps even a form of hysteria. It is quite surprising that all of the countless thousands of pilgrims who have claimed cures or betterment from the healing powers of Lourdes, fewer than 100 cases have been recognised by the Roman Catholic Church as miracles. It is easy to understand that cures which were described as miraculous at the beginning of the 20th century would not be considered such at the end of the century, due to the tremendous advances in science and medicine in the intervening years. The Catholic Church has been very cautious in dealing with possible miracles and in the 18th century Pope Benedict XIV set seven conditions to be applied to a cure before it could be proclaimed a miracle.

1 the medical condition must be serious and considered impossible to cure.
2 recovery from the condition was thought to

be quite impossible.

3 any previous treatment must be proved to have failed.

4 the cure must be sudden.

5 the cure must be comprehensive and complete.

6 there must be proof that the cure did not come about through natural means.

7 there must be no recurrence of the original illness.

A panel of doctors studies each case and the above rules are very strictly followed before a decision is made.

There are many famous stories of miraculous cures which were attributed to the healing powers at Lourdes. One concerns a man who, in his early thirties, was very seriously wounded in the First World War. After the war his health further deteriorated until he was almost totally paralysed and suffering from epilepsy. In 1923 he joined a pilgrimage to Lourdes, much against the advice of friends who thought that the journey itself would kill him. He was taken to the baths at Lourdes and then to the ceremony of sacrament. At the service he felt a sensation in his right arm and then found that he could move it for the first time in eight years. In a very short time he was walking and the epilepsy seemed to be cured. He was examined by doctors in Lourdes and, in addition to the cure of paralysis and epilepsy, there was a remarkable improvement in his war wounds. On his return to England he was able to walk again.

There are many dramatic stories similar to this and many suffering people return regularly to Lourdes believing that their conditions are at least, aided by their pilgrimage. Although the increase of knowledge in science and medicine has itself been dramatic in the past century, there is still much which man does not know or understand and the certainty of believers in miracle healing should not be dismissed as hysteria or superstition.

CHAPTER 4
SPIRITUAL HEALING PRACTICE

Many churches conduct healing services and healing is often an important and attractive part of the approach of the evangelist. Most spiritual healers however, stress that no christian faith or commitment is necessary for successful healing. The healer has the ability to channel power which, depending on the beliefs of the healer, comes from God or from nature. The patient does not even require to have faith in the healers ability to heal for the treatment to be successful. Healers do, in fact, deal with children and even animals. There are essentially two forms of spiritual healing – contact healing and absent healing.

Contact healing involves the laying on of hands. The use of touch is completely natural and is one of the oldest methods of healing and comforting. Touching brings a release of tension and a sense of confidence and reassurance. This can be seen often between a mother and child when a sore knee responds to a kiss and holding and cuddling can calm emotional upset. Common gestures such as an arm round a shoulder or holding hands expresses our care and gives comfort. The laying on of hands has the same effect as other forms of touching and the healer's hands are laid on or just above the body of the patient. The hands are usually placed on the area causing the problem and at times they are moved along the spine, a central part of the body where ailments in other parts of the body can be detected. Very often healers can make a diagnosis by using their hands and in doing so they can pinpoint the areas where energy levels have fallen because of disease. This then enables the healer to redress the imbalance by directing energy through the hands. This energy from the touch of the healer's hands often produces a feeling of heat in the affected area and the patient experiences sensations of relaxation and peace. Spiritual healers do not claim to have supernatural powers, they act as a channel for power or energy which passes through them. It is reckoned that many people have the power to heal without realising it. A man who now practices as a healer attended a service conducted by a famous healer and was introduced to her at the end of the service. As they shook hands the established healer said 'do you know that you also have the power?' He had no idea of the force within him but he gave great thought to her comment and eventually attempted to heal the child of a neighbour, with great success. He is now a healer with his own practice and is called to heal animals as well as human beings.

Absent healing is also carried out by most spiritual healers. The healing is given at a distance from the patient and can reach them at times without their knowledge. The healing forces are gathered together and channelled to the patient as a healing message. Some healers think of their current patients or pray for them at a specified time and it is not unusual for the patient to experience heat or tingling in the affected area at that time. The healer sends healing vibrations and at the same time visualises the patient in perfect health. The illness itself is not thought about in case this allows it to gather strength in the mind of the patient.

We have tended to concentrate so far on the actions of the healer but let us now pay some attention to the experience of the patient during a session of healing. Different sensations may be evident and there may also be release of traumas and difficulties related to the illness being treated. The patient needs to be reassured that such sensations are normal.

A feeling of deep relaxation often takes place leading to feelings of peace and the calming of worries and fears. The energy coming through the healer promotes this experience of calm, the face will be infused with colour and there will be increased consciousness of energy and confidence. There is often a change of temperature and there could be either perspiration or shivering. The heartbeat may be altered for a time, but this will quickly right itself. The body can feel waves passing through caused by the movement of energy and there may be a sensation of tingling. Another feeling is of muscles being gently tugged into a new position and there can even be pain in parts of the body. All of these experiences are normal and will quickly disappear.

The National Federation of Spiritual Healers (NFSH) has a register of approximately 8,000 healers and spiritual healing is an accepted therapy within the National Health Service. GPs are able to refer patients for spiritual healing and NFSH healers can visit patients in hospital if requested. It is important to have a healer with whom you are comfortable and you should therefore spend some time getting to know him or her before committing to a course of treatment. Most healers offer their services from a genuine desire to help people who are suffering or in distress. It must, however, be recognised that renumeration is often required, especially if the healer has no other way of earning. Charges are usually moderate and some healers will merely ask for a donation.

There is much scepticism regarding spiritual healing. Those who do not acknowledge the results of healing say that there is a rational, orthodox reason for an improved condition and do not accept the theory of energy or power being channelled through the healer to the patient. In spite of the prevailing scepticism, more and more people are showing interest in this form of healing and opening their minds to the subject. Because the healer only acts as a channel for the energy, it is possible that almost anyone could have the power of healing within them. The qualities required are compassion, love, patience, trust and faith in a power or energy greater than the healer's own.

CHAPTER 5
FURTHER PRACTICES AND THERAPIES

In order to understand and benefit from spiritual healing it is necessary to study various practices which contribute to and deepen the experience of healing. This involves both the healer and the patient. It is also valuable to be aware of healing philosophies other than our own, which exist throughout the world. We should always be striving to discover ways of achieving true inner peace, which is essential when approaching healing. Energy which is conveyed via the healer comes about as the product of a calm and peaceful mind. We need to set ourselves aside from the hectic pace, the cares and the confusions of our everyday life to prepare for the transmitting or receiving of healing.

Relaxation is a state which is often discussed

but which few people actually achieve. In the busy lives which we lead it is very unusual to find time to be still for half an hour, but with patience and determination we can reach a state of real relaxation. It requires discipline and thought for true success. Choose a time when you will not be disturbed (not always easy) and ensure that you are comfortably warm and wearing loose clothing. It is possible to relax either in a chair or lying down but do not become too comfortable, as this will tempt you to fall asleep! Keep your back straight as this ensures that your chest and lungs are open and your back muscles have a chance to relax. Begin relaxation by breathing deeply, using the full depth of chest and lungs. This is where the discipline takes over and you follow a script to reach complete relaxation. Turn your mind to your right foot. Feel the toes, the heel, the ankle, the shin, the calf, the knee and the top of the right thigh. Keep still and make this journey of concentration very slowly. Now think of your left foot and follow the same journey up your left leg. You should try to explore each part of your body in your mind – slowly. Complete this mental exploration of your body, including hands, arms, face, head, spine and all other parts. You should be aiming for awareness of your whole body and you will feel yourself becoming heavy. Repeat the whole process but this time tense and flex the muscles as you travel round your body. Turn your head to the left and right to release tension and then tense the muscles in your face. Again you will feel heavy and your whole body is relaxed and full of ease. Go back to the deep breathing with which you began this session and try to put all thoughts out of your head and concentrate on the breathing. You should be aiming for a state of quiet and calm but at the same time being aware of your entire body. Slowly rise to your feet and gently return to your normal pattern of life. In time, with practice, you will find that your relationship with the world around you becomes more alive, gentle and compassionate.

Meditation is the act of contemplation or reflection, especially as a religious practice. To practice meaningful meditation it is important to have quietness, a time of maximum energy and no interruptions. Early morning or evenings are good times and try to arrange soft lighting. As with relaxation, you must keep your back straight. A straight-backed chair offers the best posture although sitting cross-legged on the floor is also good if you do not find the position too difficult. The spine should be erect with the hands folded on the lap or resting on the thighs. The head should be upright and straight, the mouth closed and the eyes slightly open looking down or closed. In this position you should achieve a state of being tranquil, relaxed but aware. Ten minutes per day is long enough to allow your mind to concentrate and it will then move to contemplation and meditation. The practice of meditation can be aided by the use of deep breathing, as in relaxation.

Aura therapy is practised by healers who believe that there is a psychic body in addition to the physical body. This psychic body surrounds the physical and is a field of spiritual energy which connects to a universal source. This field is called the aura and is thought to show the state of health of a person because it is made up of radiations caused by interactions of cells and chemicals in the body. The aura can vary in distance from the body and is made up of bands of light covering the colours of the spectrum in addition to black, white and grey. The aura of each person is individual and healers who can see this manifestation claim that it helps them to detect an individual's character and mood as well as their health, physical or spiritual. The significance of the colours is as follows:

- Red signifies passion and vitality and the person concerned would be outgoing, vigorous and generous.

- Orange suggests ambition, good health and energy.

- Yellow denotes an agile mind and optimism.

- Green is a healing colour and can mean that the person has the power to heal.

- Blue means inspiration and integrity.

- Indigo is related to blue and denotes good moral values, serenity and good nature.

- Violet is a less common colour in the aura and can signify great insight and spirituality.

- White means truth, purity and perfection.

- Black represents negative thoughts and possibly reveals a person who is damaged emotionally.

- Grey can indicate illness.

The healer using aura therapy also channels spiritual energy to the aura of the patient thus altering the balance of a colour and bringing it back to normality.

A related healing method is colour therapy and is often used along with aura therapy. Colour has always been believed to have the power to affect our mind, body and spirit. Ancient civilisations used colour in their temples because of the beneficial effects which brings and today colour is still important to certain eastern philosophies. Anyone who gives thought to the decoration of their home knows that blues and greens are restful colours and easy to live with, whereas red is eye-catching and much more strident. As with aura therapy, the various colours have different properties and are reckoned to influence different ailments. The following is a rough guide to these uses:

- Red – circulation, anaemia
- Orange – the chest and the digestive system
- Yellow – nervous ailments and skin problems
- Green – stress, headaches and emotions
- Blue – fevers and nervousness
- Violet – rheumatism and epilepsy

The practitioner uses normal healing techniques to establish the causes and extent of condition he is treating. He will concentrate on the spine and, using the vibrations he receives, he will pinpoint the seat of the colour imbalance and select the colours to be used in the treatment. A colour therapy instrument beams coloured lights onto the patient, sometimes covering the whole body and at other times focussing on a specific area. Complementary colours may be used in conjunction with the principal colour appropriate to the condition. The efficacy of colour therapy has not been proved and it should only be used as complementary treatment.

It is believed that there are seven main centres of energy in the body. The name used for these centres is chakras, which in Hindu means 'wheel of fire'. These chakras are similar to terminals that can contact the healing energy and conduct it to the physical body. They are placed close to the glands of the endocrine system and to major nerve networks, which intersect the spine at specific points. They are believed to be the source of physical and spiritual energy.

There are seven chakras and the first is to be found at the base of the spine. This chakra is known as the root centre and is related to the potential of human beings, sexual activity and the primitive areas of our being.

The second chakra is situated close to the reproductive organs and is associated with sexual and creative energy and also the digestive system. It is known as the sacral or spenic chakra.

The third chakra is known as the solar plexus chakra and is associated with the spleen and pancreas. It is often reckoned to be the seat of personality and power.

The fourth chakra is the heart chakra and is located just over the heart. It is associated with the heart and circulation and relates to love and compassion.

Chakra number five is known as the throat chakra and is found at the back of the neck extending downwards to the front of the throat. It is associated with the thyroid gland and relates to communication, expression and the higher thought systems.

The sixth chakra is to be found between the eyebrows and slightly above. It is associated with the pituitary gland and it governs self-awareness, intuitive seeing, joy and the power of the mind. This chakra is of particular importance in absent healing.

The last chakra, number seven, is known as the crown chakra. It is located at the top of the head and is connected to the pineal gland. The crown chakra is associated with the brain and the highest consciousness.

The importance of the chakras is that they

are points in the body which receive and transmit energy to the body and each chakra operates on a different frequency and supplies a different area. If any of these entry points become obstructed or closed, the energy required by the body is restricted and this can lead to physical diseases.

CHAPTER 6
OTHER HEALING PHILOSOPHIES

In the past thirty or forty years many people in the western world have felt let down and disillusioned by the breakdown in traditional spiritual and moral values in the west and have turned to other philosophies which might bring them deeper fulfilment in their lives. The hippie movement and the new age movement turned to the east for alternatives to organised religion and people of a certain age will remember the journeys of the Beatles to India and their meetings with a renowned guru. The eastern philosophies have also been boosted in Britain by the large immigration from the Indian sub-continent. These philosophies appear to promote new concepts of relating to others and achieving a deeper insight and awareness of self. These ideas certainly appear to have a more acceptable plan for daily living than the materialistic self-centred society in which we live.

Buddhism is the non-theistic religion and philosophical system which was founded in north east India in the 6th century BC by Gautama Siddhartha (the Buddha). His followers seek to emulate his example of perfect morality, wisdom and compassion, leading to a transformation of consciousness known as enlightenment. Buddhism teaches that greed, hatred and delusion separate the individual from the true perfection of the nature of things. The apparent substantiality of all objects, including the self, is illusion. Ordinary things are impermanent and in the end unsatisfying. The fundamental doctrine of Buddhism was laid down by Gautama in his first discourse at Benares. The Four Noble Truths are: life is characterised by suffering, the cause of suffering is greed, to end greed is to end suffering, and the way to accomplish this is the Eightfold Path.

The components of the Eightfold Path are: right understanding, right resolve, right speech, right action, right livelihood, right effort, right mindfulness and right meditation. The path is not meant to be a step-by-step programme but an integrated spiritual attitude. It will be seen that the teachings of Buddhism lead the individual to a greater understanding of life, a striving towards enlightenment, compassion and meditation. These aims are completely in tune with the essential tenets and operation of spiritual healing. Personal development and compassion for other people are allied to meditation, and meditation is important to many forms of healing.

Zen Buddhism is practised in China and Japan and is a form of Buddhism brought from India by a monk called Bodhiharma in 520 AD. Zen is opposed to rationalism and this has gained it followers in the west. The two major sects (Soto and Rinzai) stress the use of meditation and logical paradoxes to counter the rational mind in the belief that transcendential wisdom can be encouraged and the individual can reach his own enlightenment. A great deal of Chinese and Japanese art, music, literature, calligraphy, the martial arts and even the tea ceremony came directly from the Zen vision of life. The Japanese tea ceremony (cha-no-yu) originated in China but was brought to Japan by Zen priests. The ceremony takes place in a room of simple perfection and requires humility from those taking part, who enter the tea-room on their knees. A teamaster presides over the ceremony and the object is to achieve a contemplative calm with attention being exclusively fixed on the ritual and the utensils used. The kettle, tea bowls, bamboo whisk and ladle are chosen for their artistic merit.

Hinduism is not a religion with a formal creed but is instead the complex result of about 5,000 years of continuous cultural development. The beliefs and institutions are followed by about 400 million people in India and parts of neighbouring countries. It includes a number of extremely diverse traditional beliefs and practices and has been influenced by most of the other younger religions of the world. Central to the religion is the belief that the result of a person's actions in life leads to reincarnation at a higher level of life. The aim is to find a release

from the cycle of rebirth and to return to the
ultimate unchanging reality, Brahman. Release
may come about through doing good works,
devotion to a particular god, of which there are
many, or through various types of meditation
such as samadhi, which is the state of perfect
concentration attained in deep meditation.
Ayurveda, which from Sanskrit means
'knowledge of life', is an ancient medical treatise
on the art of healing and prolonging life. As the
name suggests, this is not merely treatment for
illness when it occurs but is a code for living
which embraces all aspects of a person's life,
physical, mental and spiritual. Natural and
homeopathic medicines are used by the healer
and much emphasis is given to meditation and
rituals which aid the concentration of the
patient to blot out pain and focus on improved
wellbeing. The healer pays particular attention
to the lifestyle of the patient evaluating his diet,
the amount of exercise he takes, personal
relationships, work and any other aspects which
might provide clues of changes which would
require to be made to combat any illnesses

present and adjust harmful practices with a view to attaining a balanced and healthy life.

According to the Ayurvedic system, every living being in the universe is made up of three basic elements. These are called vata, pitta and kapha and are reckoned to control every physical and mental process.

- Vata – this is the moving force behind the other two elements and is compared to the wind. It is thought to be the most important element, influencing all actions and feelings of the body, including the nervous system, breathing, the flow of blood and the brain.

- Pitta – this is thought of as the sun and provides heat and energy. It has influence on the digestive system and also prompts ideas, opinions and the quest for knowledge.

- Kapha – this influences the balance of fluids and the growth of cells and is compared to the moon. It is important to the strength and stability of the body and is also believed to promote good emotions.

The believer in Ayurveda considers that

everyone is made up of different proportions of the three elements and the Ayurveda healer is concerned to ensure that they are all in harmony. It is said that each person is ruled by one of these elements and the healer attempts to establish which one has the ascendancy in his patient. This will determine the type of treatment to be used and what would be the best antidote from a wide range of options. There are thousands of remedies from natural sources such as minerals, herbs and vegetables and these are allied to therapies such as yoga, exercises for breathing, meditation and massage. Diet is also important in the Ayurvedic system and there are six types of food be considered -sweet, sour, bitter, salty, pungent and astringent. Food should be enjoyed, not hurried, but eaten in a relaxed fashion. Many doctors in the west accept that Ayurveda is a very good system for the promotion of healthy lifestyles and agree with its concentration on complete physical, mental and spiritual wellbeing.

In recent years there has been a rising interest in the occult and proof of this can be seen in the many books on the subject, which crowd the shelves in bookshops. Occultism is based on theories and practices which believe in hidden supernatural forces that are presumed to account for phenomena for which no rational or scientific explanation can be provided. Great store is set by ancient texts, secret rituals, esoteric traditions and the powers of the mind as keys to the understanding of life. There is a natural fear of the unknown and many people view occultism as evil and not to be approached because of this. The growth of interest in this area is, perhaps, related to the New Age movement and its ideas and perhaps to the decline of traditional religion in the developed world. There is an obsession with the meaning of life and also the foretelling of the future. Almost every newspaper and magazine carries predictions for the future, based on the stars, and an amazing number of people read these predictions avidly, some even believing them! Man is constantly striving to understand the world and universe in which he lives and there are many areas which are still outside his knowledge. Spiritual healing at least shares with occultism this attribute of not always being understandable by rational or scientific explanation and perhaps there are situations where elements of both can work together for the good of a patient.

Throughout history, witch doctors, shamans and various types of healers have been very prominent members of society. In primitive societies, they carried a great deal of authority and not without reason. The witch doctors learned the properties of herbs and potions, they developed remedies for the many ailments which affected their people and, above all, they built up belief, respect and confidence in themselves. Even modern doctors acknowledge that the relationship between doctor and patient can have a significant effect in the way the patient responds to the treatment prescribed. There are areas of knowledge in medicine where so-called witch doctors understood diseases and their treatment many hundreds of years before modern medicine caught up. Much of the treatment given witch doctors is psychological in its nature and they have been particularly successful in dealing with hysterical or psychiatric illnesses. The witch doctor established his prominent position in primitive societies because he worked for the good of his people against the evil around them and within and he used the local religious beliefs in conjunction with his knowledge of medicine. As well as his herbal remedies and perhaps massage, he would orchestrate colourful rituals and ceremonies, wearing masks and unusual costumes, which were a visual help to psychiatric doctoring. The use of chants and rituals established the authority of the witch doctor and in his healing he may also use hypnosis.

Shamanism is a religion based on the belief that the world is pervaded by good and evil spirits who can only be influenced or controlled by the shamans. The shamans were priests or medicine men of a similar religion among certain tribes of North American Indians. Many different forms of folk medicine are used in different parts of the world and so called white witches were still operating in Britain until well into the 19th century.

CHAPTER 7
THE HEALER

What type of person becomes a spiritual healer? At one time it was thought that a healer was someone of particularly great intellect or gifted in such a way that they were set apart from ordinary people. However, as we have already discussed, the National Federation of Spiritual Healers has a register of approximately 8,000 healers and it is difficult to believe that everyone on the register is a gifted intellectual! Many people discover almost by accident that they have the gift of healing and they will begin to practice while continuing their normal work as a tradesman, businessman, nurse, hairdresser or high court judge. On many occasions a person will think of the possibility of becoming a healer as a direct result of receiving spiritual healing themselves. I have told earlier of the healer who had no knowledge of his gift until he met a famous healer at a service and was told that he also had the power. The knowledge or suspicion that the power to heal may be present does not instantly produce a healer, as the person concerned has to consider matters and come to a decision whether they have the strength of mind and personality to become involved with the problems illnesses of other people. It takes courage to claim to have healing powers and one can often meet great resistance, especially from orthodox medical practitioners.

A good healer requires certain qualities such as patience, trust and belief and, ideally, a personality which will encourage calmness and confidence from the patient. Patience is needed to listen carefully and learn to understand the person receiving the healing and move ahead with the treatment at the tempo most suitable to him. Trust in himself is necessary both to reassure the patient and sustain the healer himself if the energy does not flow as expected. Belief in the power greater than his own is also imperative and he must be able to call on help

from God or the universal source in which he
believes. Confidence and assurance in himself
and his outside source of power can only be
built by time and practice. The healer must also
be observant and learn to read the reactions of
the patient. It cannot be overstressed that the
healer must be a good listener and with practice
he will learn the right questions to ask to enable
him to understand the roots of the patients
problems. It is important that he concentrates
totally on the other person's problems and prays
and asks constantly for help from outside
himself to arrive at the best possible conclusion
for the patient.

It must never be forgotten that the healer is
merely the channel for the healing energy which
will revitalise the patient's own power and set
him on the road to recovery. I have heard the
analogy of thinking of the healer as a fully
charged battery, his hands as the jump leads and
the patient as the battery needing to be
recharged. This describes the situation very well
and once the patient's battery has been
recharged he can then move forward positively

and aid his own recovery. The greatest benefits
in spiritual healing came about when there is a
real connection between the healer and the
person being healed. The healer can visualise
the energy coming from God or the universal
source down through the top of his head and so
filling his body and being transmitted to the
person receiving healing through the hands. The
energy purifies and revitalises the healer's body
and as he relaxes he allows it to flow through
him and into his patient. It should be made clear
to the patient that the healer is not there to
absorb and take on their illness and pain. The
healer is merely providing this channel of
energy and received energy will enable the
patient to assume their own power again and so
help them to regain their health. Most healers
come to their calling full of love and compassion
for those who are ill, but taking on their illness
and pain does not bring them release. On the
contrary, the healer will absorb negative energy
from the person who is ill and will be unable to
act as the channel of energy which is his real
function. Time limits should not be attached to

healing, If the healer reaches the point when he becomes a real channel and the energy is flowing in a natural way, he has then enabled the person receiving the healing to heal at their own pace. The only way to increase and improve the flow of energy and the success of the healing is to practice. The last attribute of the healer which should be mentioned is one which, if attained, will prove to be one of his greatest strengths – intuition. Intuition will come with experience and with the cultivation of his own deep inner knowledge. Meditation or a similar discipline will help in the sharpening of his intuition and it will be aided by the good listening and practice in asking the right questions which have already been referred to.

The healer must be aware that many people who come to him for treatment are unsure of what is about to happen. Some patients may have been persuaded by family or friends to try spiritual healing and are very sceptical about the possibility of a good result. It is important that lines of communication are opened up from the beginning between the healer and the person being healed. The patient must also be encouraged to relax and feel comfortable and the healer should work to banish any feelings of anxiety which are certainly likely to be there. The healer, therefore, should not just push ahead with the laying on of hands or any other treatment which he proposes to use. This is not a physical operation and the mind, spirit and feelings of both healer and patient must be fully involved. The healer must act with great sensitivity and respect.

The patient should be asked each time the healer's hands are laid on a different part of the body if he or she is comfortable about this being done. This approach helps to create an open, honest relationship, which will also aid the healer in assessing and dealing with the patients' problems. There should be a dialogue established and active co-operation from the patient undoubtedly assists in the direction of the energy to the area of the body where it is required. Treatment should not be rushed and when co-operation is working well, the healer can gain useful information in an easy and friendly manner. The person receiving the healing can be asked where the pain is, how severe it is and what type of pain they are experiencing. They can be asked about their feelings and also what they visualise during the treatment. All of this information helps to find the seat of energy blockages, enabling the positive energy to be accurately directed and the negative energy extracted. What is in fact happening is that the person is taking part in their own healing, and having questions answered and sensations and feelings described accurately is an invaluable assistance to the healer. This co-operation can be aided by taking time at the beginning of a healing session to get to know the person and find out what they expect to gain from the healing. Ask how the condition from which they are suffering has affected their life and what changes they would envisage if the condition was cured or improved. This helps the person to look ahead and see the healing as something positive which will affect their life for the better. They are then much more likely to open themselves to the healing, making the process much more straightforward for the healer.

It is important for the healer to get as much feedback from the patient as possible, especially about what they are feeling in their body. In our modern society we often find it difficult to talk openly about how we feel and, in particular, men have been encouraged to suppress their emotions and more intimate thoughts. In the hectic life which we live the healing session is often the first time for a very long period that we have the opportunity to stop, relax, clear our mind of all problems and deadlines and concentrate for a little while on ourselves. It is then that we can allow our emotions and feelings to come to the surface and we can then understand what our problems really are. It is an important function of the healer to create the atmosphere and trust which will bring about the surrender of everyday duties and problems and allow the person being healed to find themselves and truly feel an inner quietness. Many healers will use soothing music to help create the desired atmosphere, but the most powerful influence is the approach and sensitivity of the healer himself. The person being healed must therefore be encouraged to relax completely and feel, trust and talk freely to the healer. Only when these conditions have been met can the two move ahead to marshal the energy from a higher source and direct it to clear the blockages which are causing the illness.

The healer should take great care in preparing the room in which the healing session will take place. There should be pleasant, soft lighting, a bed with a clean covering, a towel, a pillow and a blanket. When the bed is not being used, the pillow can be held by the patient if he wishes and this can be comforting. Tissues should also be available, as there may be tears or noses to be blown. The person receiving healing can become cold when there is a release of energy, and then the blanket will be useful. Above all, the room to be used for a healing session should be pleasantly lit, comfortable and reassuring.

As important as the room is the composure and readiness of the healer. He must put aside any personal problems or worries and be prepared to focus totally on the person who will receive the healing. Meditation should be used to ensure that he is calm and relaxed and able to deal with his patient in an unhurried manner. It is better to work at a pace dictated by the person being healed; otherwise they may feel that they are being pressured and unconsciously withdraw their co-operation. The healer must rid himself of any reservations or criticism that he may have of the person to receive healing. It is important that he bears in mind his obligation to bring healing to all who request it and that everyone deserves respect. The necessity for the healer to be an attentive and sensitive listener cannot be overstressed. If the patient is relaxed enough to talk freely, they can often indicate, without realising it, the root of the problem which they have and the type of healing which might be appropriate. When a person becomes upset and perhaps bursts into tears, the most natural reaction is to rush to comfort them to place an arm round their shoulder or offer them a tissue. Such action can be unhelpful and should be resisted if possible. In such a situation any interruption can disrupt the flow of emotion and the opening of the person to healing. The reaction of many people to emotional comforting in these circumstances is to thank the comforter and take steps to suppress their feelings. It is possible that the healer in these circumstances has rushed to offer comfort because of his own embarrassment at the display of emotion. The correct time to offer comfort and support is at the end of the healing session when the patient will want to gain control of his emotions before leaving. The ending of a healing session is as important as the preparation at the beginning of a session and the aim should be to end the healing at a logical point and close with a warm feeling of trust and closeness. If this can be achieved it will ensure that the healing will continue after the session and the person receiving healing will look forward to the next session with confidence.

Chapter 8
THE ESSENTIALS OF HEALING

Having dwelt on the importance of various factors in the setting up and conduct of the healing session, we should now consider in greater detail the essential elements in spiritual healing. The most important element is one, which is even now not fully understood, healing energy. Energy is all around us at all times and we are all aware of the uses and properties of electricity, which is so necessary for life in the modern developed world. Even such a widely used energy is not fully understood. It is, therefore, hardly surprising that healing energy, which seems to be produced by the human body, is also difficult to explain. This energy has been used in healing down through history and many people are aware of it, some can hear it, some can see it as colours and the majority can feel it or sense it.

The energy is there but how can it be harnessed and put to use in healing? This brings us to the other essential element, which is the method used by the healer to transfer the healing energy to the body of the person receiving healing. There are instances of healers being able to direct energy to their patient through their eyes or by the use of their voice, but the most useful instrument for the transfer of energy is the hands. The hands can either stroke the body or pass over it at a distance of a few inches. Each hand has a separate function. The left hand receives energy from the higher source or draws negative energy out of the person being treated. The right hand channels and directs the energy to where it is needed. One simple exercise will demonstrate the power that can be generated by the hands. Clasp the hands together and then rub them together hard. Very quickly they will become warm and they will tingle as the healing energy is activated. Next hold your hands in front of you with the palms facing. Move the hands apart by about 18 inches and then bring them almost together. By repeating this exercise first slowly and then faster you will feel the charge of energy build up between your hands. This exercise is simply to show the presence of the healing energy and it is not needed as a preliminary to the laying on of hands. Meditation and prayer is the proper preparation for a session of spiritual healing.

Let us now consider what is liable to happen during the course of the healing session. Having set the scene properly and prepared himself mentally and spiritually, the healer is now ready to begin treatment. It cannot be stressed often enough that the function of the healer is as a channel for energy, which does not come from the healer himself, but from a higher source. The healer will not be unaffected by the energy which is flowing through him, but he must not be concerned if he does experience sensations, images or feelings which are strange to him. He is allowing a strong flow of energy through his body and this flow will undoubtedly make him more open and receptive and increase his sensitivity to others and also to himself. At first these sensations will prove disconcerting and it is natural for the healer to worry about them. It is important that he recognises from the beginning that it is usual to experience such sensations, which are manifestations of the energy that he is allowing to pass through his body. He should not be distracted by them. His task is to concentrate on the person who is receiving the healing and strive to remain a calm, quiet channel for the energy, which if properly directed, will enable the patient to heal himself. Difficult as it may seem, these manifestations must be ignored to ensure that the healer remains an open channel.

As he is working with his hands in the direction of energy, it is possible that he will become aware that his hands have left the patient's body and are passing an inch or two inches above the body. If the distance is no more than two inches the healing will not be affected, in fact it is possible to conduct the entire session this way. If the hands move further away than this, they should be moved closer. It takes experience and confidence to touch another person and that will only come with time and practice. The healer will no doubt become aware of other signs that are quite common. His hands may detect vibrations in the body of the patient and the hands themselves may vibrate. This is very usual and should cause no concern. The vibrations are caused by movement and rebalancing of energy within the body and are to be expected.

There are many other happenings and sensations which will impose themselves on the healer as he works. Images may enter his mind unbidden, which at the beginning may surprise him. He may see images of lovely countryside, colours, religious symbols or parts of the body. These are further manifestations of the openness of his body to the inflow of the external energy. As with the vibration of the hands, there should be no concern over these signs and images. Many healers become conscious of an instinct or what some describe as an inner voice telling them of the root cause of the illness that is being treated. With experience, this diagnosis from within can be insistent and can very often be correct. The healer must, however, never forget he is a channel and not a physician and must not place too much reliance on his instinct. If he suspects the presence of a serious disease, he should quietly suggest to the patient that he might be wise to have a medical examination of that area. He should do everything possible to avoid alarm and make clear that he is not a doctor. It is not always helpful to tell the patient on a regular basis what he thinks may be the cause of trouble as this may create a blockage of the healing energy in the patient. The healer should also guard against the natural tendency to impress the patient with his knowledge and strong powers of diagnosis. Experience will teach him to hold his own counsel and not cause extreme concern that is totally without foundation. In talking to the person who is receiving healing, it is important for the healer to be positive at all times.

The healer may not only detect signs and symptoms relating to his patient but also to himself. When a healer is inexperienced, it is not unusual for him to pick up signs and symptoms from his patient and actually suffer pain and distress. This can be surprising and unpleasant and can often indicate that he has become too involved with the person before him and is trying too hard. Again we must stress that the healer must remain detached and leave himself open to the flow of energy. Other signs of too much involvement are headaches and feelings of tiredness. The healer must not expect significant results from every healing session and he should not be depressed or disappointed if progress is not obvious. He must relax, take his time and not set targets for each session. A headache is usually a sign of stress or tension and more will be gained by relaxing and recharging the batteries than insisting on pushing ahead regardless. There are other very common sensations that should be regarded by the healer as normal occurrences in the healing process. He will at times perspire and feel hot or, alternatively, he may feel cold. There will also be temperature changes in the body of the patient

and these may also combine with feelings of
denseness and fluidity. These represent areas of
differing degrees of energy and do not affect the
healing process. If the balance of the body has
been upset, it is not surprising that these
differences occur. The art of healing is extremely
unpredictable and practice and experience will
demonstrate that these happenings, which
appear to be obstacles at the time, should be
ignored and the healing should be continued as
placidly as possible.

Everyone is different and the healer should
not be side-tracked by these differences. The
challenge is for the healer to remain calm and
relaxed and leave himself open to receive and
channel the healing energy from the higher
source.

Just as the healer has to be prepared for and
deal with various sensations and manifestations,
so the person receiving the healing will
experience various feelings which they will find
difficulty in recognising. The healer should
explain what might happen and reassure his
patient that these feelings are normal and

nothing to worry about. In a comfortable room with pleasant lighting and perhaps tranquil music playing in the background, the first and perhaps most welcome feeling will be that of deep relaxation. This can sometimes lead to sleep but more likely a feeling of calm and peace. If this state can be held, it will help the patient to receive the inflow of healing energy and induce a better awareness of harmony within his body. At the end of the session the patient should be dealt with sensitively and gently brought back to a normal state. After this experience he will feel calmer and more lively and confident in returning to everyday life. The inflow of energy from the healer will have reached the parts of the body that have become unbalanced and the process of healing will have started. The patient will probably experience changes of temperature similar to the healer, but for different reasons. He should be told to expect this and reassured that it is caused by the movement of the energy in his body and it will not last long. If he is shivering, the blanket can be used to warm him until the feeling passes. He may feel great heat from the healer's hands, which is evidence of the energy getting to the seat of the problem. Heat tends to indicate the release of joints in some ailments and the clearing of toxins in others. Shivering is likely to come about from a dissolving of stress or trauma, possibly associated with sighing. The patient may also sense changes in his heartbeat, but again this will pass quickly. It is not surprising that healing energy from a higher source flowing through the body of the healer and into the body of the person being healed brings feelings and sensations that are unexpected and a little worrying. The movement of the energy can move through the body like waves or feel like a weight bearing down. He may also feel vibration from the hands of the healer, tingling and even a pulling sensation from inside his body. In aggravated cases there may be pain for a period of perhaps 48 hours, caused by the energy moving into parts of the body which have been neglected or not functioning properly for some time. Rest will aid the body to return to normal. The patient may also see in his mind images and beautiful scenes similar to those which may be visualised by the healer. These visions are often bright and uplifting and may even give to the person concerned a new purpose and reason for living. At the end of a healing session the patient will possibly experience a strong feeling of liberation, having been freed from past memories, guilt or anxiety. This liberation very often has to take place before the healing of the physical ailment can really begin. The patient may be filled with a riot of emotions and he will require help and reassurance from the healer, especially as there could be a tendency to depression in some cases. The support from the healer will aid the patient in returning to normal life and pressing ahead with the healing but he should be made aware that it is his life and his body and ultimately the healing will come from him.

CHAPTER 9
FURTHER REFLECTIONS

In chapter 7 we discussed the essentials of
healing and looked at the form and operation of
a healing session. We will now consider in a little
more depth some of the questions that arise and
have to be answered and understood.

Generally speaking, there can be three types
of results from a series of healing sessions. On
some occasions there is no improvement which
is noticeable to the person receiving the healing.
This is a fairly rare occurrence and there can be
many reasons for it. The basic reason is that the
person is not able to allow themselves to be
totally open to the healing energy. But why? It
may be that at some time in their past life they
have been severely traumatised or hurt and this
is inhibiting their ability to relax and achieve the
openness and serenity which allows the healer to

channel the energy to the areas of the body which require it. Some people are intimidated by the atmosphere of a healing session and having a stranger touching them. Some may have lived with their problem for so long that they are actually afraid to take steps towards a healing. It is almost like a fear of the unknown. It does happen at times that a person who has received healing feels no improvement and is dejected and disappointed. Then, perhaps weeks later, they begin to notice a change in their condition and find that they are able to face their problems in a much calmer and more confident fashion.

The second type of result is the one which happens most often – partial healing. People who report partial healing will probably have experienced the sensation of energy movement during the healing session and afterwards will find some relief of their problem, but not a complete healing. It is to be hoped that some of the people who have received partial healing will return for more treatment. The fact that the participation in the session will be much more familiar to them a second time will, perhaps, enable them to open fully to the healing energy, this time with better results.

The final type of result is a complete healing. Complete healing of relatively minor illnesses happen regularly and many healers have an excellent record in this area. These illnesses may be muscle pain, headaches, pains in joints or other general aches. The reputation of a healer who can produce regular success in the area will quickly spread and he will be kept very busy. A complete healing of serious illnesses such as cancer or arthritis is much less common and requires much longer healing and careful preparation by the person receiving the healing. This preparation would include changes in diet, counselling, meditation and prayer. The patient in these circumstances is doing everything possible to clear the way for the healing energy and they will be able to reach a state of equilibrium and calm.

Although we have considered three types of healing of varying success, it should be remembered that the vast majority of people who receive healing feel different afterwards.

They will have experienced some sensation of the movement of the energy during the session, and in the days following some changes, either in their health or in their general attitude to their everyday living.

The above examination of the various degrees of healing highlights the most important element in spiritual healing. The healer has to be accomplished in channelling energy and moving it to the part of the body where it is required. He must also be 'good with people' and be able to create the atmosphere in which the healing can flourish. To be a spiritual healer one must be spiritual, and the healer should be in constant contact with his God or divine inspiration through prayer or meditation. Another element in the healing is the type of illness and the gravity of the illness. The patient suffering from a serious illness may, through fear, create major blockages to the receipt of the healing energy. On the other hand, it is often the case that there is more resistance from a patient with a minor ailment than on with a serious illness. The more serious the illness, the more preparation is required from both healer and patient. The final element, therefore, in the healing is the person receiving the healing. He must, first of all, want to be healed. If we assume that is indeed the case, he should do everything he can to be in the best mental state for the healing session. It is just as important for the patient to prepare himself as it is for the healer. He should be open and relaxed and confident in the skills of the healer. He should also be prepared to remove all obstacles to the flow of healing energy and let his negative feelings and emotions go.

Questions, which are often asked, are 'why is healing at times associated with pain?' and 'how long does healing take?' The healing process can often create feelings of pain or anguish as the energy within the patient's body moves to regain balance. Old wounds are uncovered and these can be emotional, mental or physical. The emotional traumas are the most common and the hardest to deal with. They may have been caused in childhood or early life and the person may not even have realised that they were still there. In order to get rid of such injuries, the patient should be helped to confront the hurt, as this is the only way to clear it from the system and allow the healing energy to enter and do its work.

The length of time required for healing is almost impossible to estimate and, in fact, no time limit should be applied, as this in itself can create resistance to the healing and slow down the whole process. There can be healing which moves ahead quite quickly and the rate of healing is obvious to both the healer and the patient by a noticeable shift and movement of the energy in the body. Alternatively, a healing session can result in a healing process that may progress slowly and almost unnoticed for days, weeks and even years. The patient should be advised that there will be no rush with the healing and that it will move ahead at the pace which is most suitable to him. The more relaxed and secure the patient feels, the easier it will be for the healing to progress to a conclusion.

The healer must make an assessment of the type of illness with which he will have to deal.

One type is very straightforward. If the illness or injury has been caused by external forces – perhaps a burn, an accident affecting a limb, an infection – then the healer can see the problem quite easily and can proceed with healing immediately. If the illness has originated inside the body, more investigation and questioning may be necessary. Many illnesses can develop as a result of previous events which have produced trauma, fear, anger or hurt, leading to energy being locked in the body.

Strange as it may seem, pain and distress as well as being destructive and stressful, can at times be signals which are passing the message that something is wrong. Forces in the body are out of balance and energy blockages have occurred. The causes of such blockages may have taken place many years before and the patient may not be aware of them. It is important for the healer to probe and question until the root causes becomes clearer. It may relate to the loss of a parent in childhood or a broken relationship in later life. It may be a loss of self-esteem at some stage, due to a failure, which the patient now does not want to acknowledge or confront. Whatever the cause, it must be found before real healing can take place. The healer, in a very kindly way, must question the person receiving the healing and help him to uncover the basic problem and release deep emotions that are causing it. The result of such deep introspection can be distressing, resulting in even sobbing or crying, but the release can open the floodgate of emotions and create the conditions that will allow healing to begin. Most people have suffered some pain or trauma in the past which has lodged with them, even though they may not be aware of it. An instinctive action of self-preservation is to shut down the thoughts and memories of the cause of the pain in an attempt to retain self-control. This may work for a while but the resultant energy blockages lead inevitably to illness in later life. It is easy to understand that people who have had horrific experiences such as trauma in war or have been victims of violent crime or child abuse can trigger such shut downs, but the same automatic response can affect people who appear to have had a fairly placid life. It is common for many people to refuse to accept that they have a problem and this creates a real challenge for the healer. It is also possible that the person can be unsure of their inner feelings and the cause of their problems leading to signs of confusion within themselves. All of these possible causes of energy blockage have to be understood and probed by the healer before real healing can begin.

We will now consider the importance of the mind in our illness and our health. The conscious mind is programmed by our experiences in childhood and adulthood and produces our ideas and opinions and judgements, based on information received from the subconscious mind. The conscious mind deals with the here and now. In spite of its programming, the conscious mind does accept new information and changes in experience and it is helpful during a healing session to accentuate any improvement in energy shifts and release, as this information will have a positive effect on the conscious mind. The subconscious mind is the library of all memories, tastes, sounds, smells and sensations which we have experienced during our life. With practice, the healer can access the subconscious mind and change some of the emotions which have been rooted there. This can be done through good co-operation with the patient and through his understanding and assimilation of the positive changes that are being suggested. Then there is the part of the mind which is in contact with God or the source of life energy. The importance of this part of the mind to the healer is tremendous and the connection must be kept open by regular prayer and meditation.

The mind has a major part to play in the condition of a person's health. It can at times be the cause of illness and it can also have a decisive effect in the curing of an illness. There has always been an understanding that when a person is mentally or emotionally 'low', they are more prone to illness. We have all known times when we have been low and have fallen victim to colds and various headaches and pains which would never have bothered us if our state of mind had been positive and confident. It is well understood that many people are well below par during the dark winter months and they are more likely at that time to suffer illness of all kinds. It is thought that the shortness of the days and the resulting lack of light has a significant effect on many people, making them feel listless, requiring more sleep than usual and generally feeling down. In the words of an old song 'life gets tasteless, don't it?' It would appear that many of the major events that happen during life have the power to reduce the resistance to illness and disease. These include the death of a spouse, another near relation or a loved one, divorce and even moving house. Major happy events such as marriage or having a baby can also, surprisingly, lower resistance to illness. It would appear that any major change affecting a person can affect the mind and then reacts to affect the body. If the mind is in a negative state it can pull the body down with it. There are many instances of a person dying soon after the death of their spouse or after being told that they have a terminal illness. There is no obvious physical reason for this happening and it seems that the will to live disappears and the body takes the massage from the mind. Scientific research is being done to try to establish the reasons for the physical reaction to the highs and the lows of the mind. None, however, seriously disputes the fact that a person is more susceptible to illness when their mind and spirit is low and that those who are of a cheerful disposition can often throw off illness.

The mind also plays its part in what is probably one of the most common and most widespread conditions in present day life, stress. There is no doubt that stress is a condition that has affected mankind throughout history, but it has assumed a particular importance and recognition in recent years. Our modern lifestyle is blamed for the apparent rise of this illness and it is certainly true that the competitive nature of life, long working hours and the general sense of job insecurity have all contributed to a stressful atmosphere. Stress can affect the mind in many different ways. Concentration and memory can be affected, as can moods and energy. People who are normally of a cheerful disposition can become bad tempered and there can also be a constant feeling of exhaustion. Stress can also induce physical ailments and aches and pains, which are now seen as danger signals from the mind to indicate that something is wrong and must be addressed. Doctors have known for many years that certain illnesses and diseases are directly related to stress. The most common ones are heart trouble, high blood pressure and breathlessness, although it is thought that there may be many other disorders, which come from the same source. Stress, therefore, is not just a feeling of being under pressure with the associated symptoms such as anxiety, difficulty in sleeping and the inability to relax. It can also trigger serious diseases such as diabetes and cancer. Counselling is being used more and more to combat stress, especially for people such as firemen, police and survivors of disasters who have had particularly horrific experiences. This can be of help to many people but it is the case that many of the signs and symptoms recognised by doctors do not originate in the body, but in the mind. When this has been diagnosed the patient should turn to other therapies which can help, such as spiritual healing. The healer has the time and the skills, with the co-operation of the patient, to explore the energy blockages and shut down emotions, which have probably been made worse by the stress. When the patient has finally opened himself up the healing can then proceed. The healer can also lead the person receiving the healing to other therapies, which may be beneficial, such as relaxation, meditation and also physical exercise. There is a range of illnesses, which were labelled psychosomatic, or, in other words, 'all in the mind.' In recent years modern science has challenged the idea that these illnesses are imaginary and it is now being recognised that, except in people suffering from hypochondria, they are ailments with real causes. Among these illnesses are asthma, eczema and allergies. All of these can be helped by spiritual healing.

We have looked at how the mind can react

and influence illness, let us now consider how
the mind can influence good health. It is now
accepted that the mind can have a positive effect
on the working of the body, especially when
allied to exercise and a healthy and balanced
diet. If a person can do everything possible to
maintain a happy attitude to life they are likely
to aid their body in fighting illness and disease
and keep their body in balance. It is a facile
thing to say that everyone should be cheery. We
all have different natures, and many of us do not
find it easy to look on the bright side. Younger
people who have not yet had the experience of
the harder side of life find it much easier to be
carefree and happy than those who are older
and have had that experience. We will all have
our share of sadness and stress, which will affect
our mental state and our general health, but we
should seriously strive to be positive of mind
and relax as much as possible. It is said that
some stress is good for us but we should try to
keep it within bounds as it can have such a
negative effect on both mind and body. We have
already discussed meditation and relaxation and

it is a good idea to build these into a regular routine. If time is put aside for these disciplines, there will be a positive gain in mental outlook, a general feeling of better health and the knowledge that the body is much more in balance. Even when things are not going well and illness occurs, it is undoubtedly true that a happy and cheerful disposition will aid a quicker recovery than a miserable one. There are various methods for treating the mind when it is disturbed such as hypnosis, psychotherapy and psychoanalysis. They can be very effective in correcting disorders of the mind, but very often they can produce results with illnesses and diseases which are seen to have a psychological cause. Much has still to be discovered about the workings of the mind, but it is already evident that it can be a powerful agent in keeping the body healthy as well as combating illness.

CHAPTER 10

RELATED HEALING

Folk Medicine

In modern times folk medicine has come to embrace all care for the sick by healers who are not recognised as doctors and who practice both herbal and magical medicine. Folk medicine goes back to the beginning of time and the roots of the practices used are considered in earlier chapters. It has continued to flourish side-by-side with modern orthodox medicine and many people in the scientific medical area have shown increasing interest in folk medicine during the past 50 years. This medicine of the people has origins in the mists of time and there are references to it as far back as 2000 BC in Egypt, 1200 BC in India and about 500 AD in Persia. This early medicine used magic and religious rites but also developed the use of herbs and mineral extracts. It is probable that in the beginning all illnesses were treated by the shaman or witch doctor, who had general knowledge of most diseases but, in time, the healers began to specialise. The increasing specialisation of Egyptian doctors was noted by the Greek historian Herodotus and it is generally agreed that the type of scientific medicine which we know today was first practised by Hippocratic, the Greek physician, in the 4th century BC. The advance of medicine was extremely slow after the fall of Rome and the rise of Christianity. The first medical schools in Europe were established in the 11th and 12th centuries in Salerno in Italy and Montpellier in France. The traditional healers did, however, continued to deal with the vast majority of cases requiring treatment.

Although folk healers are not recognised as doctors, they learn their craft by observing and imitating experienced healers in their community, perhaps shamans or witch doctors, and very often healing is believed to be a gift bestowed on one family and is passed down

from father to son or mother to daughter.
Whereas spiritual or faith healers use touch and
prayer to treat illnesses, other folk healers will
tend to invoke magical rituals, charms, massage
or rubbing, infusions of herbal teas or mixtures
of vegetables or organs from animals. There are
also many superstitions and traditional rites,
such as pulling the patient through the fork in a
tree or a bush to get rid of an illness.

It is surprising how similar many of the
treatments used folk healers throughout the
world can be. Some of the ideas of the ancient
Greek healers are still retained, among them the
belief in certain balances in the body, such as the
equilibrium which should be maintained
between hot and cold, moist and dry and
external and internal pressure. If the essential
balances of the body are not maintained then
disease will occur. The healing practices used by
the Chinese, the American Indians, in Europe
and in various primitive cultures are remarkably
similar to the early medicine of the Western
world and even to the alternative medicine of
today. Until fairly recent times, the American

Indians drove out the demons of disease by the use of songs and incantations and they also used herbal medicines, many of which are now used as drugs in modern scientific medicine. The Chinese also use magical, herbal and religious treatments and cures and, in addition, other therapies such as acupuncture, meditation and introspective therapy. They would appear now to be experimenting with bringing these traditional methods into a combination with modern scientific medicine.

In days gone by it was believed that disease was caused by evil spirits and demons, the modern equivalents being germs, viruses and bugs! Some of the traditional folk treatments are now being used again as alternatives or as complements to modern medicine and many physicians are turning their attention to a more holistic approach to finding cures.

Holistic Medicine

Holistic Medicine embraces the idea that the patient should be addressed as a whole person who is affected by all factors in his lifestyle-physical, emotional, mental and spiritual. Diet and exercise are also factors which contribute to the total make-up of the individual. The patient's environment must also be taken into consideration. The various treatments which are given, along with the advice on healthy living, should enable the person concerned to be actively involved in the supervision and control of their own health. In recent years the holistic movement has experienced a remarkable increase in interest and acceptance and it is at present undergoing great change and development. Holistic medicine does not have a universal approach to diagnostic procedure or treatment but can embrace all types of medical practices, including spiritual healing, folk medicine and the normal testing and laboratory methods used in modern medicine. The holistic practitioner can also turn to acupuncture, meditation, fluid replacement, psychic healing, hypnosis and a host of other ancient and modern therapies and disciplines. He has, indeed, a powerful armoury in the war against disease!

The diagnosis by a holistic healer may include modern scientific testing and may also advocate the use of certain drugs, but the physical, spiritual and mental factors involved will be paramount to the decision which he comes to regarding treatment. The major drive behind holistic thinking is to use the person's own self-healing power and tap the unique strength in their genetic, biological and psychological make-up. Although surgery and scientific medicine will be used when required, the main emphasis will always be fixed on healing of the whole body and any corrections which may be needed to diet and lifestyle. Education regarding health and all aspects of care for the body are part of the holistic approach and the need for preventative self-care is emphasised Holistic medicine has a very positive attitude to health and the promotion of this attitude is causing interest among physicians involved in cancer therapy. They are trying to encourage their patients to think much more positively about treatments such as chemotherapy and radiation therapy. A major holistic technique is touching and this is used in many therapies such as massage, chiropractic manipulation. This physical contact, in addition to the direct healing it provides, also brings greater relaxation and enhances sensory awareness. Psychotherapeutic bodywork is another holistic health therapy which has influenced the field of bioenergetics. An illness is looked on not only as a negative event but also as an opportunity for innovation and progress. Holistic medicine recognises that events in a person's life such as the death of a close relative or friend, divorce or sudden unemployment can lead to a break-down in health.

In recent times many traditionally trained doctors have looked in depth at the ideals and benefits of holistic medicine and have encouraged physicians in the mainstream to join in the all-encompassing approach of the holistic idea.

Christian Science

In 1879 Christian Science was founded by Mary Baker Eddy, based on the teachings laid out in her book *Science and Health*. In 1892 she established in Boston the Mother Church, First Church of Christ, Scientist. The denomination accepts many of the basic tenets of Christianity, including belief in one God, the life and teachings of Jesus and the authority of the bible, but disagrees with the belief in Jesus as the Son of God, viewing him essentially as an example of the divine sonship of God which is part of all mankind. Christian Science also considers that redemption in the Christian sense is a rising from the physical into the spiritual. The world of matter is not created by God and diseases and illnesses are not related to the spiritual side of life. Mary Baker Eddy wrote that 'We must have trials and self-denials, as well as joys and victories, until all error is destroyed.'

A board of trustees is at the head of the church, although the branches throughout the world have an independence which is established in the framework laid out in the

Manual of the Mother Church which was published in 1895.

There are about 3,000 branches of the church in 57 countries throughout the world, although the vast majority are in the United States. Christian Science practitioners carry out a full-time healing ministry that stresses the importance of prayer in the treatment of disease. This is considered an essential step on the way to salvation. Unlike some other sects, the followers of Christian Science are not instructed by the church to use prayer exclusively and many do use traditional doctors in serious cases. The congregations use the bible and Mary Baker Eddy's book *Science and Health* as the cornerstones of their services of worship and also have reading rooms available for study of the books. Their regular meetings also include the sharing of healing experiences among the members of the congregation. The newspaper of the denomination – *The Christian Science Monitor* – is a very highly respected paper in the United States, although many of its readers may well not fully understand the beliefs, objects and history of the church which owns it.

The founder of Christian Science, Mary Baker Eddy, was born on a farm near Concord, New Hampshire, in 1821. She was a most remarkable woman who was described by Mark Twain as 'the most daring and masculine woman that has appeared on the earth in centuries'. Her childhood was marred by poor health and she was greatly affected by the death of her mother in 1849. Her father was a very strict Calvinist and the relationship between the two was very difficult. She was given to violent temper tantrums and hysteria. Her first husband died and her second marriage ended in divorce in 1873. A man who made a profound impression on her was Phineas Parkhurst Quimby, who was an American spiritual healer. He was a mental and spiritual healer and also used hypnosis in his healing. He eventually came to the belief that cures came about through the discovery of truth and that he had uncovered the healing methods of Jesus. Mary Baker Eddy became a disciple of Quimby's and his theories obviously influenced her thinking. She appeared to have a miraculous recovery from a severe fall and this experience led her to devote years of thought and study of the bible, leading to her book, which became the basis of Christian Science. Asa Gilbert Eddy was one of the people who was drawn to her at this time and in 1877. Mary Baker Eddy continued to lead the Christian Science until her death in 1910.

Scientology

This is a strange sect that was founded in the 1950's by L Ron Hubbard. Hubbard had been a prolific writer of cheap pulp novels and then he launched his book *Dianetics*, which set out a new type of psychotherapy. Although not an easy book to read, it purported to expound a system of beliefs and therapeutic practices which demonstrate the influence of holistic medicine and certain Eastern religions, as well as Freudian psychology. A further range of turgid volumes followed. The movement was widely criticised for the financial demands that it made on its followers, but in spite of this, it established itself in the UK and in other countries in addition to its main base in the United States. In the early 1980's Hubbard was accused of financial mis-management and he died in 1986. The author has twice visited the cult's luxurious headquarters in Hollywood, California and well remembers the strange reception area, complete with the baby grand piano and white feather boa!

CHAPTER 11

THE POSITIVE ATTITUDE

Any investigation of healing of any kind, whether it be spiritual healing, folk or holistic medicine or any of the other types or forms of healing which have been examined in previous chapters, reveals the importance of the relationship between mind and body. The power of the mind cannot be exaggerated and the state of mind of a healer is of great significance both to the person receiving the healing and the healer himself. If the healer's mind is not at ease and in positive mode, there is little chance that healing will take place. Much more is now known about the mind, but still it's versatility and power constantly surprise and amaze the experts. If a person sets their mind to anything it is more than likely that they will be successful and, alternatively, if negative attitudes are dominating the mind, success will be much harder to achieve. It is important for us to learn how to develop positive attitudes, as the ability to do this will bring better healing results and also improvements in our own mental attitudes and general health. The positive mental approach gives a good start to taking control of our own health and establishing responsibility for our own lives.

Recent research has shown how mental attitudes can affect health in a very direct way. There appears to be a link between negative mental attitudes and some types of cancer and a higher incidence of cancer in the later years in people who have experienced feelings of low personal esteem, resentment, self-pity, the lack of ability to release anger and tension. Most people now also recognise the fact that those who experience high levels of stress in their lives are susceptible to high blood pressure and heart disease. In the lives which many of us live, it is not possible to avoid tension and stress and we must, therefore, take steps to counter the effects of our modern lifestyle. It is possible to change our attitudes and so improve our health. We should work on eliminating negative feelings of self-pity, anger and guilt and substitute them with positive feelings of self-respect, optimism and love. Increased consideration for other people will help to get rid of feelings of anger, envy and frustration and the other negative impulses that can affect the mind and also our moods.

We have acknowledged that we must work at arriving at a more positive frame of mind and we may have to develop techniques to enable us to do this. If we are serious in our desire to be more positive, a good start is to turn to meditation. The techniques of relaxation and meditation will create a condition of mind which will facilitate the concentration which is essential to the aim of arriving at a more positive state of mind. We must be prepared to use our imagination and release the immense power of the mind. This use of the imagination is not a new concept. We have mentioned earlier that the cult of Asclepius in Greece required the patient to spend a night in an incubation temple, believing that the gods would effect a cure in a dream. The patient was purified and his dreams were interpreted by the priests, with a view to formulating care and treatment for the ailment. We do not have to visit a temple in Greece in order to exercise our imagination. When unable to sleep, we have all tried to concentrate on a scene or a place where we have been happy and where we can find peace. By using that kind of concentration we can also work at ridding our mind of the negative thoughts and emotions and replacing them with positive feelings. There is no need to spend hours in meditation and concentration like a monk or a guru; in fact, better results can be obtained by using this technique in short periods on a regular basis. The imagination can affect the body as well as the mind. Think of a lemon and then think of biting into that lemon and almost certainly the saliva will begin to flow in your mouth! These exercises of imagination can be used by a healer when dealing with a patient. To activate the process the healer suggests an image on which the patient should focus, such as the affected area of their body being bombarded by white light or a stiffness being gently heated and relaxed by the summer sun. If the images being suggested by the healer do not appeal to the patient, they can be asked to suggest their own.

It is clear that effective healing has many components. The healer must harness all of his healing powers to be able to open himself as a channel for the healing energy and he must also bring together the various attributes required, such as patience, understanding, a positive mental attitude and a genuine belief in what he is doing. In his book *The Power of Positive Thinking*, Norman Peale stated that a positive response could come about from the use of a positive mind, prayer, faith and affirmations. What are affirmations? The dictionary defines them as 'statements of the existence or truth of something'. In the context of healing, they are statements to ourselves that we are getting better. The technique of affirmation was developed by a Frenchman, Emile Coue, at the end of the nineteenth century and produced a phrase now known to many – 'Every day, in every way, I am getting better and better'. This autosuggestion is an aid to the imagination and to the attainment of a positive mind. The theory is that, with regular repetition, it becomes lodged in the mind and encourages the mind and the body to create harmony, which in turn will fight disease. Affirmations are not prayer. Prayer is not a repetition of set phrases – or certainly should not be. Prayer should be a dialogue with whichever God you believe in. Christianity teaches that we should pray to God as our Father and this is a relationship that is easily understood. We should not pray as though making affirmations, but rather as conducting a conversation with someone who is well known to us. People who use prayer on a regular basis and really think about what they are saying are constantly surprised by how often their prayers are answered, although perhaps not in the way they expected.

The techniques described in this chapter are not complicated, but require deep thought and consideration. The healer should ponder them and practice them before attempting to use them in a healing session and he will find them much more effective once he has established a good relationship with his patient.

CHAPTER 12
THE MIND AND HYPNOSIS

We have seen how a positive attitude in the mind can affect a person's whole lifestyle and it is abundantly clear that the mind is a powerful healer. It is no longer true to think that health is outwith the control of the individual and that all treatment must rely on drugs. It is perhaps a little surprising that scientific medicine has taken so long to investigate and explain the vast range and power of the mind and to understand how it can best be used.

The first physician who seriously undertook the task was an Austrian called Franz Anton Mesmer. He discovered how to place his patients into a trance-like state, from which he claimed to be able to carry out some very surprising cures. He also introduced a new word to the language – mesmerise 'to hold someone as if spellbound'. Mesmer called his new treatment 'animal magnetism' and he believed that the results which he had in effecting cures were brought about by the transfer of magnetism from himself or his equipment. He claimed that this transfer of magnetism restored the bodily balance of his patients. Mesmer was criticised for his claims by his colleagues in Austria but he was much sought after in France, where one of his patients was Marie Antoinette, the wife of King Louis XVI. His new healing methods caused a great deal of controversy and eventually the king set up a royal commission to investigate the claims for animal magnetism. This was in 1784 and the American Ambassador to France, Benjamin Franklin, was appointed head of the commission. After taking evidence from many people who had been helped by the treatment given by Mesmer, and in spite of some very interesting evidence, the commission found that there was no evidence of magnetism in the cases which had been examined and decided that the cures which had been achieved had been as the result of pure imagination. One member of the commission, Dr Antoine Laurent de Jussieu, disagreed with the other members of the commission and issued a minority report stating that Dr Mesmer's treatment had, indeed, induced a trance in his patients which had produced cures which could not be explained. This report was very damaging to Mesmer and his career as a healer soon came to an end.

The healing career of Franz Anton Mesmer may have come to as end, but there was still considerable interest in his methods. John Elliotson, one of the founders of University College Hospital in London, had seen a demonstration of mesmerism in France and realised that it could have a use in the area of controlling pain during surgery. He studied the methods of Mesmer and before long he was mesmerising his own patients and performing operations, including amputations, without anaesthetic and with great success. Around 1840 a doctor called James Braid came up with a new word to replace mesmerism, which still had associations in the minds of many people with fraud, superstition and stage performances. The word, which he coined, was 'hypnosis', which the dictionary now defines as 'an artificially induced state of relaxation and concentration in which deeper parts of the mind become more accessible: used clinically to reduce reaction to pain'. In the mid nineteenth century, a doctor with the East India Company, James Esdaile, read an article on the new technique called hypnosis and decided to try this new approach to avoiding the pain of surgery. It is said that he experimented first on a convict and after that initial success he went on to carry out thousands of operations in India over the next decade. The fame of these operations greatly impressed the government of Bengal and they gave him charge of a small hospital in Calcutta, which was named the Mesmeric Hospital. All of this success did not impress many of Esdaile's colleagues in the medical profession and he was actually expelled from the British Medical Society. He did share many of Mesmer's original ideas on the technique and seemed not to understand the importance and power of the mind during a trance.

It must be remembered that this experimentation with mesmerism, which became hypnosis, took place before the discovery of anaesthetics and the surgical operations carried out, using mesmerism, by the likes of Esdaile were really quite remarkable. Today hypnosis is widely and successfully used by surgeons, psychotherapists and dentists. It can be used as an anaesthetic or to relieve anxiety, to relax the patient and so reduce resistance to therapy, to aid memory and even to treat certain conditions. Hypnosis is used on some occasions to help the patient stop smoking, cut down on the amount they eat, or counter fears such as the fear of flying. No matter how the technique is used, it should only be carried out by trained therapists. We will now look at hypnosis as a therapy in a little more detail.

It is amazing to think that hypnosis is such a strange phenomenon that no completely satisfactory definition has yet been developed for it. The British and American Medical Associations have defined it at present as 'a temporary condition of altered attention in the subject that may be induced by another person'. There is still a great deal to be understood about hypnosis, even concerning the state of the brain reaction during treatment. A person under hypnosis appears to be asleep, but scientists have found that the brain wave patterns seem to be much closer to the patterns of deep relaxation. Hypnosis is now considered to be a form of attentive, receptive and highly focused concentration, which is able to ignore any external and peripheral events that may be taking place.

The remarkable feature of the hypnotic trance is that the person under hypnosis can become easily influenced by the suggestions of others- normally the hypnotist. Although they can appear to act in a normal manner and can walk, talk, speak and answer questions, their perceptions can be greatly altered or distorted by external suggestions. At the command of the hypnotist, the subject may lose feeling in a limb, feel no pain, experience an altered heart rate or a change in temperature. They can experience visual or auditory hallucinations or even regress in mental age and live the past as if it were the present. It is this last aspect of hypnosis that lends itself to stage performances in which the subject is often held up to ridicule and which certain audiences seem to enjoy. The patient who has been hypnotised may forget all or part of what happened during the trance and they can also be made to remember things that they had hitherto forgotten. The hypnotist may make posthypnotic suggestions, which are instructions to the patient to respond to a specified signal at some time after the end of the trance. Under such instructions, it is possible for the patient to once again resume the hypnotic state on the prearranged signal. This method of treatment is sometimes used to repress or eliminate such symptoms as anxiety or headaches.

The state of hypnosis is mainly brought about by inducing deep relaxation and focused concentration. The patient becomes unresponsive to normal types of stimulation and, although he is told to sleep, he is also instructed to listen and be ready to react to commands or suggestions given to him by the hypnotist. Under the trance the patient tends to be more amenable to these commands and suggestions than would normally be the case, even if the instructions are illogical and completely out of character with his normal conduct. It is interesting to note, however, that it is not possible to make a subject carry out commands which seriously conflict with his moral sense. Even if directly commanded, it is certainly unlikely that the person under hypnosis will emerge from the trance ready to commit murder or robbery.

The normal methods used to induce a hypnotic trance are usually simple and mainly use repeated commands and monotonous suggestions repeated again and again. The patient is asked to concentrate on the voice of the hypnotist, fix their eyes on one object or listen to a repetitive sound. He is told over and over again that his eyelids are growing heavier and heavier and that he is feeling drowsy and relaxed. He is invited to go into a deep sleep. The time taken to induce a trance rarely takes longer than a few minutes and, on occasions, only a few seconds. If it is suggested to a patient during hypnosis that it will be easy to be hypnotised again, he will usually go straight into a trance immediately on an agreed signal from the hypnotist. The hypnotist will usually awaken the patient by ordering him to return to his normal state and telling him that he will feel well and alert after the trance. Some patients can for a short time feel disoriented and drowsy after a trance. Many experts are of the opinion that patients are more likely to succumb to hypnosis if they have confidence and belief in the hypnotist, but the factors which bring about hypnotic susceptibility are, even now, far from being fully understood. There is evidence that a good subject for hypnosis tends not to be of an anxious disposition, but rather someone who is interested in new experiences, imaginative and intelligent. There is still a great deal of disagreement regarding the exact nature of hypnosis with some medical experts claiming that it is possible to hypnotise any patient and others thinking that hypnosis is often brought about by the eagerness of the patient to please the hypnotist and their willingness to explore an unusual experience. Whatever the answer is, there is no doubting the fact that this strange and powerful therapy has a very real contribution to make to healing.

CHAPTER 13
SELF HEALING

If we are interested in healing, and possibly in practising healing on other people, it would appear reasonable to spend a little time in considering what healing we can bring to our own body and how we can improve and take responsibility for our own body. Nowadays we are constantly bombarded with advice on diet, exercise and the conduct of our lifestyle – a term which was quite unknown until recent years!

It was Robert Burns who said:

> *O wad some Power the giftie gie us*
> *To see oursels as ithers see us!*

Before embarking on attempting to heal or advise other people, we should have a good long look at ourselves to see what requires healing in our own body and lifestyle. Most of us now know that changes in diet and the taking of more exercise can make huge differences to how we look and how we feel and we surely owe it to our prospective patients to look and feel as good as possible. Let us look first of all at how we eat. It has often been said that our body is a machine that requires fuel to enable it to work. The fuel is, of course, the food, which we eat, and the drink, which we take. Car drivers know that if they use inferior fuel in their car, they will get inferior performance and, in the same way, if we eat and drink inferior foods and liquids we will have a similar result with our bodies. Many people these days appear to allow insufficient time in their day to think about what they will eat or how they will prepare it. Instead of looking forward to and preparing good fresh food, they reach for and consume convenience and fast foods that are almost invariably high in fat content, artificial colouring and the dreaded E numbers! Ensure that you start the day with a good breakfast of cereal, bread or fruit and try to make time in the middle of the day for a lunch that you enjoy. Sit down and relax for a minute or two! It is important that you top up your energy levels for the afternoon. Try not to have too large an evening meal and again consider the fat content of what you are eating. Snacks are not really a good idea as they are very high in fat. Bear in mind that most potato crisps contain 65 per cent fat and peanuts are even higher. It would, perhaps, be a good idea to slow down your supermarket shopping and read as many labels as possible. Most of us do not drink enough water and it is important to try to rectify this as water contains all the minerals required by our body and also helps to flush away the impurities. Enjoying our favourite alcoholic drink is one of the pleasures of life, but ensure that this is done in moderation as the body has to work very hard to get rid of the toxins produced and over indulgence does not leave any of us feeling fresh and healthy!

The lives that we lead at the beginning of the 21st century do not leave very much time for exercise. In days gone by people walked everywhere and every day and probably had all the exercise they needed without thinking about it. Now we have the motor car and public transport and distractions unknown in previous years, such as television and computers. It is a fact that even children do not play physical games as before and many of them are in danger of becoming too fat! More and more people are now trying to put aside more time for exercise, with the result that gyms and health centres are appearing everywhere at a very health rate. One of the most accessible forms of exercise is walking. It is a good natural exercise, which has the added advantage of providing the opportunity to enjoy fresh air. A reasonably brisk walk is preferable to a saunter and it may help to remember that the British Army marches at 4 miles per hour with full pack. The full pack is not required in civilian life. The problem with walking is, of course, the British weather and this is where the health centre comes into its own. It is possible to lay aside a little time each day or each week for the treadmill, the cycle or the rowing machine without disrupting our life and the benefits will soon become apparent. Exercise should not be an endurance test, in fact, the experts say that you should be able to exercise and carry on a conversation at the same time.

The need to allow time in our lives for exercise is also true for other aspects of our lifestyle. It is all a question of organisation and to be a complete person we must make time for leisure and relaxation. The ability to relax properly is not easy and requires planning. Do not slump in front of the television every evening. TV has its place in our lives, but don't let it take over. You will be surprised how relaxing it is and how much better you will feel if you listen to some music, read a chapter or two of a book or indulge in your favourite hobby for some time during an evening. During the weekend get out and about, even if it is only for a potter in the garden. One of the most used words in the language these days is 'stress'. There is no doubt that there is a great deal of it about, probably mainly caused by the constant pressure to earn a living and the apparent lack of security of employment with which to do it. Stress can lead to many other undesirable circumstances and situations. The tension which comes with stress so often leads to anger and conflict and it can also damage love. If problems arise, try to keep your feelings under control and give yourself time to think things through coolly. If the problem is a personal one involving another person, try to talk through the difficulties rather than keeping your anger and frustration to yourself. Repressed anger only increases internal tension, which can actually lead to illness. As someone once said in a famous song 'give love a chance'. We should no more keep our love to ourselves than our anger. Be positive. Let those whom you love know this on a regular basis and, between you, you will create an ambience of love which will defuse many of the disagreements and conflicts which arise in any relationship. A spiritual aspect to your life will also bring stability and even a serenity that will prepare you to participate in life as a useful and positive person. If you can effectively heal yourself and achieve a truly positive outlook on life you will be much more prepared to approach the calling of a healer.

CHAPTER 14
THE POWER OF LOVE

In the previous chapter we touched on the strength and positive influence of love in everyday life. We will now look at the nature of love. Love is one of the most used words in the language and features in most popular songs and greetings cards. It is used very often without thought and certainly without reference to its real meaning.

Of all the invisible forces and energies at work in the world, love is perhaps the widest, deepest and strongest and it is also the most dominant in the field of spiritual healing. We have discussed the various techniques used in spiritual healing, the auras, the flow of energy which is so central to the healing, the philosophies and the beliefs which all come together when a healer lays his hands on a person wishing to be healed. Is it possible that love is, in fact, the most powerful influence of all? When one thinks of the love of a mother or father for a child, a grandparent for a grandchild or the other forms of selfless love which manifest themselves in the human heart and soul, is it not also possible to think that the same selfless love for another is in the heart and soul of a healer as he approaches a person awaiting healing? Healers do not become healers to make money but to share their gift of healing and, if possible, improve the health of another human being. Many healers take no payment for the treatment which they give and most others will only accept the cost of expenses. They are, above all, genuine healers who want to share their gift because of their compassion for their fellow human beings. One healer has said 'you cannot measure love in a laboratory, but you can measure its effect on other people'.

It has long been known that the general health of a happily married couple tends to be better than that of a couple with a less marriage or someone who is single. Various researchers have explored this curious fact and they have all had to agree. The reason would appear to be that the constant support and love of a partner help to reduce the effects of the stress of everyday living. It is often the case that the survivor of a long and happy marriage lives a very short time after the death of the person who has shared his or her life.

The same advantages to health have also been ascribed a person who has a long spiritual commitment and attachment to a religion or a firm belief in God. These people appear to have a more stable and contented life than the average, with lower rates of suicide, drugs abuse, divorce and depression and also greater marital happiness.

It is heartening to know in this troubled world that the most powerful influence of all is that of compassion and love and that this diverse power can be used in so many ways for the benefit of mankind, including the power to heal in the hands of a spiritual healer.

CHAPTER 15
BIOLOGICAL ENERGY

Whenever spiritual healing is discussed or written about, as in this book, there is constant reference to energy, whether the energy deployed by the healer or the energy naturally present within the body. This energy is the core of healing and it links up with the chakras, which we have already considered, the auras, meridians and other points in the map of the body. The energy, which is present within the body, is known as biological energy and more and more scientists are now studying this essential but little understood life force. Modern scientists are now aware that many of the ancient ideas on biological energy and the treatments arising from them should be re-evaluated, as many of them are being found to be totally in accord with up-to-date scientific study.

In an earlier chapter we touched on the ancient Ayurvedic healing tradition in India, which was probably the oldest system known for the treatment of disease and the promotion of health. In the second chapter of Genesis is written:

And the Lord God formed man of the dust of the ground, and breathed into his nostrils the breath of life; and man became a living soul.

This breath of life which appears in this very old book of the bible is the prana of the Ayurvedic tradition, which in ancient Hindu teachings is described as one of the basic elements of the universe and is a power which comes from the divine being. We are born with prana and our good health depends on this breath, or energy, flowing undisturbed through our body. A plentiful supply of prana ensures the balance required for good health, but if this balance is upset, the prana is also blocked, leading to disease and bad health. The channels or entrance points by which the universal energy enters the body during spiritual healing are known as chakras, which we have looked at previously. The prana can be affected by many factors, including mental attitudes and stress. If we can harness the prana, it is then possible to begin to heal ourselves and also others.

In ancient Chinese medicine, the yin and yang are contrasting but complementary principles. Yin is the negative feminine mode, associated with the earth, darkness and passivity, whereas Yang is the positive masculine energy associated with heaven and light. The principles of yin and yang are important to Taoism, which emerged in the 6th century BC. Taoism is one of the two major Chinese religio-philosophical movements, the other being Confucianism. The aim of Taoism as a philosophy is profound, joyful, mystical and practical harmony with the universe. In making his way in life, the follower of Taoism will seek the path of least resistance and of inconspicuousness. He will believe that all extreme positions revert to their opposites, yin balances yang and everything is in flux except

Tao, which means 'the Way'. Meditation, spontaneity and simplicity are very important and as a religion Taoism seeks a formula for immortality by breath control, diet, sexual continence and exercises, known as tai chi. The Chinese word for prana or energy is Ch'i. The Ch'i enters the body via the meridians or chakras and science now seems to suggest that these channels are, in fact, the collagen fibres of the connective tissues. These tissues are between the main organs and provide a system of fibres, which run throughout the whole body, creating a connective structure that can act as a conductor medium. There is, therefore, something similar to an electrical circuit reaching to all parts of the body and this is the circuit which is accessed by acupuncture by way of the meridians. Before moving on to consider the use of acupuncture as a treatment, it is worth mentioning another Chinese discipline, which is, perhaps, less well known than some others. Tai Ch'i is fairly popular and it can bring benefits to health. Chigung also uses the power of Ch'i and is based on the theory of the meridians, as is acupuncture. Practitioners of Chigung, through meditation and control of breath, are able to monitor the flow of Ch'i through the meridians and channels of their own bodies and can eventually learn to produce Ch'i, which can be used to treat others whose energies have been diminished.

Acupuncture is a traditional Chinese system of healing in which thin metal needles are inserted into selected parts of the body in order to access the meridians and channels. The needles are stimulated either electrically or by manual rotation. Acupuncture points can also be stimulated by pressure, ultrasound and certain wavelengths of light. The treatment is used in the Far East to relieve pain and in China as an anaesthetic. Acupuncture dates back to 2500 BC and relates to balancing the opposing life forces yin and yang. Research in the West suggests that the needles activate deep sensory nerves, causing the release of endorphins, which are natural painkillers. The ancient Chinese system was based on the theory that the two opposite forces in the body, yin and yang, could be kept in balance by acupuncture, thus promoting health and controlling disease. Many modern scientists have not been able to accept the idea of a meridian system in the body, but they have shown that the acupuncture points are more richly supplied with nerve endings than the surrounding skin areas. The treatment received a major boost, particularly in the United States, during a visit by President Richard Nixon to China. A newspaper correspondent who was accompanying Nixon on the trip required an emergency appendix operation during the visit and he reported on the pain relief, which he experienced through acupuncture after his operation. Acupuncture is being investigated by modern scientists and as far back as the 1950's a Dr Reinhold Voll created the science of electro-acupuncture. One of Voll's interesting findings was that most of the Chinese acupuncture points are to be found by a change in skin resistance and they are located amazingly close to the places described in the ancient texts. The interest in acupuncture is growing and the time may come when it will be more warmly embraced by modern science and medicine.

CHAPTER 16
THE THERAPY OF LIGHT

The importance of light in our lives is sometimes overlooked. It is not only true that light affects our moods and feelings, it is also essential to our health and general wellbeing. The famous US biochemist, Albert Szent-Gyorgi, who was born in Hungary, stated that 'all the energy we take into our bodies is derived from the sun'. The point he was making was that the light from the sun produces photosynthesis in plants, the leaves of the plants are in turn eaten by animals and the animals are then eaten by carnivorous animals, such as human beings. He came to the conclusion that enzymes and hormones in the body are affected by light and also by colour changes. As this is true, it is then obvious that if a human being is deprived of light, their health will be very materially affected. A fairly mild example of this is the way our moods can influenced by light or the lack of it. We can often be depressed on a dark winter's day and filled with joy and optimism on a bright day in early spring.

The ancient ayurvedic healing system in India held the theory that a lack of colour entering the body adversely affected health. They believed that the colour produced by light shining though a precious coloured gem had beneficial effects on the skin and tissues. The main gems, their colours and effects are as follows:

Carnelian
  colour – orange
  effect – cooling, moist and settling
Citrine
  colour – yellow
  effect – stimulating, purifying and war
Emerald
  colour – green
  effect – cold and analgesic

Ruby
> colour – red
> effect – arousing, amplifying and warming

Sapphire
> colour – blue
> effect – soothing, calming and analgesic

Topaz
> colour – white
> effect – antiseptic, fulfilling and cool

In gem therapy, combinations of gems are often used and various combinations are said to have specific properties. For instance, it is said that emerald and sapphire together are calming, cooling and analgesic and that ruby and diamond can stimulate the flow of blood and increase warmth. As in other therapies, modern technology is being introduced to the ancient healing systems and electronics are now adding pulsed frequency to the healing rays of gem therapy, with what would appear to be beneficial effects. It is claimed that when emerald and sapphire light is beamed into the head of a patient suffering from stress a dreamlike trance is achieved which can have dramatic and helpful results. This combination of old and new therapies can even be used to open up the chakras and develop treatment which is as powerful, and safer, than modern drug therapies. Modern technology is, therefore, emphasising the validity and existence of the chakras and employing a new twist to an old method of healing. Under the ayurvedic system in India, gems were used to produce elixirs that contained the individual properties of the gems, and again modern technology has been able to reproduce these elixirs by using lamps instead of the sun to create the healing liquid.

A therapy, which is related to gem therapy, is colour healing. We have touched on this therapy in an earlier chapter, but we will now look at it in more detail. Colour healing involves shining coloured lights onto the part of the body requiring treatment and each colour has individual properties which, it is said, can treat specific ailments. Practitioners of colour healing also have a strong affinity to aura healing and the two therapies are often used together. The use of colour in healing is again a therapy which goes back many thousands of years and it is thought that both the Greeks and the Egyptians chose colours very carefully for the decoration of their temples, believing that the right colours in the right places would have beneficial effects on the mind, body and spirit. This type of healing is still used in India and Tibet, and it is interesting that Buddhist monks wear orange or saffron robes because of the spiritual connotations of the colour. There is no doubt that colour can affect mood. A room which is decorated in greens and blues tends to be calm and serene and the same cannot be said for a room decorated in red and black! In colour healing it is believed that illnesses can be treated by directing colour onto the body and adjusting the input. The closeness with aura therapy is illustrated by the fact that both forms of healing believe that the electromagnetic energy of light is absorbed by the body, thus producing an aura of energy that vibrates to a pattern. When the balance of the pattern or aura is disturbed, the body is unhealthy and disease occurs. The colour practitioner then attempts to redress the imbalance by matching the vibrations in the body to the vibrations in the colour being used and so extracting the vibrations which are the cause of the imbalance.

During the first examination by a colour healer, he will establish the details of the patient's way of life and also his medical background. At this stage he will also find out about favourite colours and how the patient reacts to various colours. He will then concentrate on the immediate problem that has brought the person to him and make a detailed examination of the spine, which is very important in colour therapy. It is thought that each of the 24 vertebrae in the spinal column relates to a different part of the body and also to a specific colour. The examination of the spine is carried out to establish where the imbalance in colour is occurring, thus letting the healer know which colours to use in the treatment. The colours selected are beamed onto the body by a special instrument, sometimes focusing on the spot which appears to be the seat of the imbalance and at other times bathing the whole body in colour. The sessions of colour therapy may be spread over several weeks but the healer will also advise on techniques that can be practised at home. Through a form of relaxation and meditation, the person being healed will be taught to visualise the healing colour for their ailment, decorate their home in helpful colours and even dress in colours that will alleviate their condition. Let us look at the properties of the colours used in this form of therapy. There are many similarities to the properties that were referred to when considering gem therapy.

Blue

This is considered to be the most useful colour in healing. Blue is a calming colour and is said to help in cleansing and purifying the aura. It is said to induce peace and serenity and it is used in the treatment of depression, nerves, insomnia and all problems of the spirit, mind and body.

Green

Green is also a soothing colour and it has a very

natural feel to it. It is, of course, the colour of the countryside and is perhaps, the easiest to visualise. How many of us when under stress will think of green meadows and rolling hills and, perhaps, focus on a peaceful scene known to us and where we have been happy and relaxed? It is said that green with yellow and a little purple can balance the whole nervous system. It is used to treat heart problems, blood pressure and all ailments of the nervous system, including fear, frustration and anger.

Purple
This is a colour that brings with it a feeling of optimism and hope for the future. It is said to renew not only the spirit but also the mind and body, and it is, therefore, a versatile and much used colour used on its own and also with other colours. Its main uses are with the senses of smell, sight and hearing, inflammation and physical pain.

Gold
This is reckoned to be almost a venerated colour

that ranks at a spiritual level. It is often used in combination with other colours to produce special healing. It is used to aid the expansion of awareness, wisdom and peace, and can also help with concentration and clarity of thought.

Yellow

This is another colour, which can affect and heal the mind and soul, while helping with the achievement of a state of meditation. It also has a good influence on the nervous system and stimulates the mind. It is used in cases of arthritis, skin complaints and aids digestion.

Pink

A subdued and restful colour, pink is very calming and can create a peaceful atmosphere in the home. It can help to clear the mind and has a positive effect when applied to strained personal relationships. It is also used in the treatment of heart problems and aggression.

Orange

Orange is the colour of vitality and it is said that

it is able to clear blockages of energy in the chakras and meridians. It is employed to condition the whole body and specifically treat ailments such as asthma, chest complaints, depression and even fear and loneliness. The fact that this colour can open up the chakras to allow the flow of energy makes it especially important in spiritual healing.

Red

Red is the opposite of colours like blue and green as it is anything but soothing and is said to release adrenaline into the bloodstream, thus producing extra vitality. It is beneficial to circulation and, as a result, it can raise the temperature of the body when the patient has poor circulation. In addition to circulation, red is used to treat rheumatism, anaemia and all manner of nervous disorders.

Violet

This is another spiritual colour, which is very positive, and a great aid to meditation. It is attractive to healers and can also appeal to creative people, such as musicians and painters. Its use in healing is in the treatment of rheumatism, neuralgia and epilepsy, as well as an aid to relaxation.

We mentioned earlier the close relationship between colour healing and the understanding of the aura. The practitioners of colour therapy are said to be able to detect colours in the auras of patients and to be able to introduce beneficial colours as required. This is a more advanced healing process and needs the ability to see or sense the aura before going ahead with colour therapy. A reassuring thought is that no harm can be done by the use of colour healing, as the application of an inappropriate colour will merely fail to trigger a reaction, without doing any damage.

Although not strictly in the field of healing, the use of colour in the home can be beneficial to health and no one can deny that colour co-ordination in the home is fashionable these days. The thoughtful use of colour in the home is a real aid in creating an atmosphere conducive to comfortable everyday living. Some of the following suggestions may not suit your taste but they may spur you to think again about the colours that you use.

The first impression given when entering your home is the welcome or lack of it from the hall or entrance. The use of red in this area, either in the carpet or in decorations or pictures will produce a feeling of welcome and warmth. The kitchen is a working area and needs colours such as blue or green to give a feeling of calm and peace. This is a good area in which to introduce plants that do not encroach on the working space. The lounge is for relaxation and it is a good idea to decorate the walls in neutral or pastel shades and reserve the use of colour for ornaments and pictures. This gives the opportunity to change the atmosphere and ambience of the room without resorting to wholescale redecoration. When adding decorations to the room, do not forget coloured glass ornaments and coloured candles which, when lit, give a real feeling of peace to a room. Bedrooms should also be in peaceful colours but some excitement can be introduced by using colours such as orange or violet in pictures, lamps or dried flowers. Do not forget that other functional room, the bathroom. It is very easy nowadays to get co-ordinating colours in towels, curtains and other accessories and doing this can make all the difference. This last passage is not intended to be a guide to DIY, but rather a few suggestions which may help you to create within your home an atmosphere of peace and calm which has a definite influence on your everyday living and health.

CHAPTER 17
HERBAL REMEDIES

Spiritual healers often advise their patients on the use of certain herbal remedies which complement the healing they are receiving. This is a genuine holistic approach to the treatment and can be effective in speeding up recovery.

The use of herbs as medicine goes back into the mists of time. The ancient Egyptians were the first to make records of the beneficial properties of herbs and it is known that Egyptian priests practised herbal medicine. Records go back as far as 1500 BC but the use of herbs goes much further back. Herbal medicine was important to the ancient Greeks and Romans and was also used in China and India. The use of herbs in Britain was initially linked to monasteries, which established herb gardens to produce herbs to be used in cooking, as well as in medicine. Many healers in Britain knew and understood the use of herbs and eventually the first book on the subject was printed in the late 15th century. Herbal medicine was certainly the most popular form of treatment until the 19th century when what we now know as orthodox medicine began to gain in popularity. This medicine was based on increased scientific knowledge and in the cities it overtook the old reliance on herbs. Herbal medicine continued to be strong in the country and was part of local folklore. In recent years there has been a growing resistance to orthodox medicine with its increased use of synthetic drugs and a general unease with the huge medical and pharmaceutical industries. No doubt all of this was partially driven by green policies and green politics. In common with spiritual healing and other so-called complementary therapies, the interest in herbal medicine has also been rising in developed western countries. In undeveloped countries herbal medicine is much more prevalent than orthodox medicine.

It is not our intention to discuss herbal

medicine in any detail, but it is true that many spiritual healers have some interest in and knowledge of the subject. The following is a list of the more commonly used herbs and a short description of their uses.

Aconite

The common names are Wolfsbane, blue rocket, friar's cap or monkshood. This plant grows in the Alps and Pyrenees and was known in England before 1000 AD. The leaves are used fresh and the root is dried to be used as a treatment for tonsillitis, heart spasm and catarrh. This is a poisonous plant and should not be used without expert advice. Used as a tincture or liniment.

Anemone pulsatilla

The common names are Pasque flower, meadow anemone or wind flower. This flower is found in limestone and chalk areas. It is distilled with water to produce a fluid extract of oil of anemone for the treatment of bronchitis, whooping cough and asthma.

Balm

The common names are sweet balm, lemon balm or honey plant. This is a common garden plant, which was introduced into England many years ago. It is used as an infusion or tea for the treatment of colds or fever, sometimes along with other herbs.

Belladonna

The common names are deadly nightshade, black cherry, great morel or devil's herb. Belladonna grows in England but originates in central and Southern Europe. It is a very poisonous plant and must only be used with expert advice. It is used in the treatment of neuralgia, sciatica, rheumatism and gout. It is produced as a fluid extract and can also be incorporated in plasters and ointments.

Broom

The common names are broom tops, basam, brum, bream or green broom. Broom is to be found on heathland throughout Britain, Europe and the north of Asia. The tops are made into an infusion or a juice and in combination with agrimony and dandelion root is used for liver, bladder and kidney ailments.

Chamomile *or* Camomile

This plant grows wild throughout Britain. It has been used as a medicine since the time of the ancient Egyptians and can alleviate a large number of conditions. The flowers are used to make an infusion, fluid extract or an essential oil and applied externally it relieves pain, neuralgia and inflammation. It is a strong antiseptic and is therefore valuable for reducing swelling of the face caused by an abscess. As chamomile tea it has a powerful soothing effect and it can also be used as a tincture for the treatment of diarrhoea in children.

Clover, Red

Also known as Trefoil or purple clover, this plant is found throughout Britain and Europe. As an infusion or fluid extract it is very good for the treatment of whooping cough or bronchitis.

Coltsfoot

Coltsfoot has many common names including coughwort, horsehoof and fieldhove. It grows wild in all parts of Britain and the leaves, flowers and roots are used to make syrup or are dried for smoking. It is a popular cough remedy and along with other herbs, it is made into a herb tobacco, which is reputed to alleviate catarrh, bronchitis, asthma and lung complaints.

Comfrey

It is native to Europe and the more temperate parts of Asia but is also found near rivers and ditches throughout England. It has many common names including knitbone, bruisewort, gum plant and blackwort. It is mainly used as a decoction or liquid extract as a gentle treatment for intestinal trouble, diarrhoea and dysentery. As a tea it can be used to treat internal bleeding in the lungs, stomach and bowels and also haemorrhoids. It is also sometimes made into a poultice to reduce swelling and aid healing of cuts, ulcers and abscesses.

Dandelion

This very common flower is found in pastures, fields and waste ground in all northern, temperate zones. The roots and leaves are the basis of fluid extract, decoction, infusion, tincture and juice and also a solid extract. It is most useful when dealing with ailments of the liver and kidneys and can be a mild laxative or an aid to better appetite and digestion. It is usually combined with other herbs. The roasted root can be used as a substitute for coffee and can alleviate the symptoms of gout, rheumatism and dyspepsia.

Elder

The shrubs or small trees in the Elder family are found throughout Europe and Britain and are known by many names such as black elder, pipe tree and bore tree. Elder is extremely useful in herbal medicine and all parts of the plant are used – the bark, leaves, flowers and berries. The bark provides a strong purgative and as a tincture it relieves asthmatic symptoms and croup in children. The leaves are the basis of green elder ointment, which is used to treat haemorrhoids, sprains, bruises and chilblains and can be applied to wounds. The elder flowers are either distilled or dried. The distilled elder flower water is used in lotions for the eyes and skin. The dried flowers are infused to make elder flower tea which is a gentle laxative and is an old-fashioned cure for colds and influenza, when taken hot before going to bed.

Fennel

Fennel grows in temperate areas of Europe, the Mediterranean, Russia, India and Iran. It is better known in Britain as a herb to be used in cooking but the seeds and leaves are used in herbal medicine. It is mostly used to reduce griping when purgatives are employed and the seeds form part of the compound liquorice powder. Fennel water is also used to reduce flatulence in infants.

Foxglove

A plant, which is found throughout Britain and Europe and is known by many names, such as witch's gloves, dead men's bells, fairy's glove, bloody fingers and fair women's plant. The digitalis, which is produced from the dried leaves, is a heart stimulant that raises the blood pressure, slows the pulse and permits increased blood flow and delivery of nutrients to the heart. Digitalis can accumulate in the body and turn poisonous and must, therefore, be used only under medical supervision.

Ginseng

The Chinese have for many centuries believed that ginseng is a cure for many illnesses and even that has the powers to prolong life and restore it after death. The name of the genus to which the plant belongs is 'panax', which comes from a Greek word meaning 'to heal'. The word panacea comes from the same Greek word and means 'a cure for all ills'. Western medical scientists have been unable to find any medicinal value in ginseng, although legends and superstitions about the plant have existed for centuries. The Chinese believe that ginseng is an aphrodisiac and no doubt part of the reason for this is the strange shapes which the roots of the plant take on, many resembling parts of the human body. Fantastic tales have been told about how the roots have been able to move under the earth in order to avoid capture and how the plants have been protected by wild animals.

Ginseng has a sweet taste and a pleasant aroma and is grown mainly in North America and Asia. It is found in thick, cool woods as far north as Quebec and Manitoba all the way south to the Gulf Coast. Most of the ginseng roots grown in North America are dried and exported to Hong Kong and from there it is distributed throughout south east Asia. The plant is native to Manchuria and Korea, but is also now grown in Japan. Some users are of the opinion that Asian ginseng is of a higher quality than that grown in North America. The plant requires rich soil and adequate shade and is usually grown in small gardens, where nearly all the work is done by hand. Ginseng seeds require about five to seven years to develop fully.

Golden Rod

Golden Rod is found wild in woods in Britain
and many other areas of the world and is also a
well-known garden plant. It is also known as
woundwort and Aaron's Rod. The leaves are
used to produce a fluid extract, infusion or spray
and are very effective in curing gravel and
urinary stones. The herb aids digestion, stops
sickness and is excellent against diphtheria. As a
warm tea it is helpful with painful menstruation.

Hemlock

This is a poisonous plant that is found in
hedges, meadows and along riverbanks. It has
many names, such as spotted conebane, poison
hemlock, vex, poison parsley and spotted
hemlock. It is used for teething, cramp and
muscle spasms of the larynx and gullet. As an
inhalation it relieves coughs, bronchitis and
asthma. One of the constituents of the leaves
works as an antidote to strychnine poisoning
and similar poisons. Hemlock itself is very
dangerous and must be used with extreme care.
Antidotes to hemlock poisoning are tannic acid,

coffee, mustard and castor oil.

Honeysuckle

This plant is very common throughout Britain and Europe and the dried flowers and leaves are used to produce a syrup or decoction. The syrup is used for respiratory illnesses and asthma and a decoction of the leaves is a laxative, is used in gargles, and is effective against diseases of the liver and spleen.

Juniper

This is a common native British shrub that is also found in many parts of the world. Oil of juniper is produced from the ripe berries and is used in the treatment of indigestion, flatulence and kidney and bladder ailments. The most important use of juniper is in combating dropsy.

Larch

This tree is indigenous to central Europe and was introduced into Britain in the mid-17th century. The inner bark is used to produce a fluid extract or syrup. Its main use is as a stimulant expectorant in chronic bronchitis also for the treatment of internal bleeding and cystitis.

Liquorice

This is a shrub which is native to south east Europe and south west Asia, but has been cultivated in Britain. The root is used and is administered as a powder, a fluid extract, an infusion or as a solid extract. It is a popular and common remedy for coughs and chest complaints and the extract is included in cough lozenges and pastilles, in combination with expectorants and sedatives. An infusion of the bruised root and linseed is good in dealing with irritable coughs, sore throats and laryngitis. It is used much more in herbal medicine in China and the Far East. Liquorice is used by brewers to colour porter and stout, by the tobacco industry in the manufacture of chewing or smoking tobacco and by manufacturing confectioners.

Meadowsweet

This is a common British wild plant, which is

mainly found growing in meadows and woods. It is also known as meadsweet, dolloff, bridewort and lady of the meadow. The herb is produced as an infusion or decoction and is used as treatment against diarrhoea, blood disorders and stomach troubles. It is thought to be very good for diarrhoea in children and dropsy. The decoction has been used in wine to reduce fever and the infusion makes an enjoyable drink when sweetened with honey. Meadowsweet is also an ingredient in many herb beers.

Nettle

The nettle is found in most parts of the world in its common and stinging forms. It is used as an infusion, a decoction, a juice, a dried herb or as a herb for eating. It is used against asthma and the juice will relieve bronchial and asthmatic problems. Nettles are used very often in cooking and find themselves in tea, beer, juice, puddings and also used as a vegetable. A hair tonic can be made from nettles and, rather surprisingly, they were at one time used as a cure for insomnia in the Highlands of Scotland. The leaves were chopped, added to egg white and applied to the temples,

Opium

The dried juice from the immature seedpods of the opium poppy is the narcotic drug called opium. The term narcotic covers the group of drugs such as opium and morphine that produce numbness and stupor. When used as a medicine opium deadens pain, but if taken indiscriminately or over a long period it eventually damages physical health, brings about mental deterioration and normally results in addiction.

Opium poppies, with their fragile flowers of red, white or purple, thrive in a hot climate. After blooming, the milky juice is collected from the pods. After exposure to the air the white juice turns brown and congeals into cakes or bricks which may then be made into a powder or treated further.

Opium is mainly cultivated in Asia and the two major producing and exporting countries in the world are India and Turkey. Huge quantities of opium are still used for medicine, although synthetic drugs are now available as substitutes. The legitimate uses of opium include purified alkaloids such as morphine and codeine and alkaloid derivatives such as laudanum and apomorphine. Opium was used as a medicine as early as the days of the Assyrians and its cultivation slowly spread through Greece and Mesopotamia and reached China around the 7th century AD. During the 18th and 19th centuries almost all painkillers used throughout the world were derived from opium, but around the middle of the 19th century the danger of addiction became more widely known and laws were enacted to make the use of the drug illegal, except for medical reasons. Opiates are now only prescribed for the treatment of pain, diarrhoea and coughs.

Peppermint
This plant is also known as brandy mint, curled mint and balm mint and grows widely in Britain, usually in damp areas and waste ground. It can be produced as distilled water, an

infusion, spirit, oil and fluid extract. Oil of peppermint, especially, is used widely in medicine and has many other uses in the manufacture of drinks, sweets and foodstuffs. The oil is good in dealing with dyspepsia, colic, abdominal cramps and flatulence and it is also used as a flavour in other medicines. Peppermint water is extensively used to raise body temperature and induce perspiration. At an early stage of colds and influenza peppermint tea is useful and it can also calm heart palpitations and help to reduce the appetite.

Primrose

This is a very common wild flower, which is found throughout Britain, and the root and the whole herb are used. It can be made into an infusion, a tincture, powdered root and an ointment. In times gone by, primrose was thought to be an important medicine in the treatment of paralysis, gout and muscular rheumatism. Restlessness and insomnia can be successfully treated by a tincture of the plant and this tincture is also a sedative. An infusion of the root of this adaptable plant can ease nervous headaches and the powdered root serves as an emetic. An infusion of primrose flowers is also very good in dealing with nervous headaches and the ointment made from the leaves of the plant can soothe and heal cuts and abrasions.

Ragwort

This widely distributed and profuse wild plant is called by many names, such as St James's wort, stinking nanny, ragweed, dog standard, cankerwort, stammerwort and fireweed. It can be used as a poultice, an infusion and a decoction. The leaves were made into emollient poultices which when applied reduced inflammation and the swelling of joints. Ragwort can be used as a wash for burns, sores, ulcers and inflammation of the eyes and it has also been successful in alleviating the symptoms of rheumatism, sciatica and gout. Throats and mouths can be gargled with Ragwort and a decoction of the root is said to help internal bruising and wounds. Precaution must be taken in rural areas, as it is poisonous to cattle and perhaps sheep.

Rosemary
Although rosemary is native to the area of the Mediterranean, it has been cultivated as a garden plant in Britain since before the end of the first millennium. It is also known as polar plant, compass weed, compass plant and romero. Tea made from rosemary can help with headaches, colic, colds and nervous diseases and it is also thought to lift nervous depression. The plant can be produced as an infusion, oil and a lotion. The oil is said to cure many types of headache and as a hair lotion it is said to prevent baldness and the formation of dandruff. The oil is also added to liniments to import fragrance and to stimulate.

Sorrel
This is a plant which has long been native to Britain, although it probably originated in Eurasia and North America. It has many common names such as green sauce, sour grabs,

sour suds, cuckoo sorrow and gowke-meat. In the forms of expressed juice, decoction, poultice and dried leaves it can be used to combat various disorders and medical conditions. As a cooling drink it is useful in all conditions of fever and was used to stop bleeding. The decoction was used to cure jaundice, ulcerated bowel and gravel and stones in the kidney. It was said the sorrel juice and vinegar could cure ringworm.

Tansy

This is a hardy perennial plant, which is found throughout Britain, usually on waste ground. Tansy is produced in various forms such as oil, infusion, poultice, fresh leaves and solid extract. It is mainly used to expel worms from children and also to counter slight fevers and spasms. When tansy essential oil is used in small doses it can help with epilepsy and when used externally can help some eruptive diseases of the skin. Bruised fresh leaves can reduce swelling and relieve sprains.

Thyme

Thyme is cultivated all across northern Europe and it is used as a fluid extract, an essential oil and an infusion. Thyme is normally used in conjunction with other ingredients in herbal medicine but the fresh herb, in a syrup, is a good and safe cure for whooping cough. The infusion or tea is also good for whooping cough but, in addition, it is also helpful in the treatment of catarrh, sore throat, wind spasms and colic. It can also alleviate the symptoms of fevers and colds.

Valerian

This is a plant that is found throughout Europe and northern Asia and is common in England near rivers, ditches and marshy thickets. The root of valerian is used and produces a tincture, a fluid extract, essential oil and expressed juice. The herb is not narcotic and therefore can be used in cases of nervous debility and irritation. The expressed juice is used in insomnia and in the treatment of epilepsy and the oil has uses with cholera and in strengthening eyesight.

Witch hazel

This is a tree or shrub which is native to north America and is also known as spotted alder, winterbloom and snapping hazelnut. Witch hazel is successful in treating internal and external bleeding and also haemorrhoids or piles. It is normally used as a poultice for bruises, swelling and inflammation but is also helpful with diarrhoea, dysentery and mucous discharges. The decoction is used against a range of conditions, including tuberculosis and gonorrhoea. The tea made from the bark or leaves is helpful with bleeding of the stomach and bowel ailments and can also be given as an injection for bleeding piles or haemorrhoids. Witch hazel is extremely versatile and it can be used to treat varicose veins, alleviate the pain in burns, scalds, insect and mosquito bites and reduce inflammation of the eyelids.

CHAPTER 18
HEALING – SPIRITUAL AND ORTHODOX

In one of the earlier chapters in this book we have attempted to trace the origins and the development of spiritual healing down through the centuries. It is a fact that healing has been an integral part of human life from the very beginning, which means that the history of healing literally spans thousands of years. For most of time the healing function has been carried out by healers in the community, whether it be a settlement, a village, a tribe or small groups of nomadic people. From the beginning the healer was seen as being different and was slightly set apart as a witch doctor, a shaman, or the old woman in the village who was believed to have a power, and to whom everyone turned in time of illness or trouble. We have seen how the power to heal grew under differing religions and philosophies in the different parts of the world. The majority of healers have been religious people of one kind or another but there has always been a goodly number with no obvious religious connections.

As far back as 500 BC there was an understanding of the importance of rest, diet and fresh air to a healthy life and Hippocrates recognised the healing properties of the laying on of hands. He founded his own school of medicine and his influence on medical science lasted until the 18th century. Hippocrates is often considered to be the father of scientific medicine and doctors still subscribe to what is called the Hippocratic Oath. Over the intervening years scientific discoveries were made which shed new light on the treatment of illnesses and diseases, but it was not until almost the middle of the 19th century that what we now know as orthodox medicine began to make significant advances in the understanding and treatment of diseases. As in other facets of life and other discoveries, the rate of change in medicine has been breathtaking in the past 150 years, both in the development of new drugs and medicines and in advances in the knowledge and techniques of surgery. This explosion of medical science has coincided with the industrial revolution and the much more materialistic attitude that has resulted from it. The position of the doctor in society has also been improved and during most of the 20th century the local doctor was looked on as a person of knowledge and authority. I well remember the tidying of the house and the laying out of clean towels for the visit of the doctor!

We have noted earlier that the popularity and influence of spiritual healing has gone in cycles through the years and the 20th century was definitely a downward cycle. Hippocrates was credited with the theory that the mind and body were separate and this was reinforced in the middle of the 17th century by Rene Descartes. Descartes was one of the most original thinkers of all time and one of his influential theories was dualism. He considered that the world was made up of two different kinds of substance – mind and matter. Neither he nor anyone else has ever satisfactorily answered the problem of how mind and matter can interact. All of this concentration on the separation of mind and body has acted against spiritual healing, which lays great store by the influence of the mind on the body and the holistic approach to healing. During the past one hundred years, scepticism has been very pronounced against the idea of importance of the mind to the working of the body and the action of the individual. The word psychosomatic describes disorders, such as stomach ulcers, which are thought to be caused by or aggravated by psychological factors, such as stress. Some doctors still reject this causal effect of the mind on the body, but an increasing number recognise the connection and agree to its existence and the need for treatment of the root cause. There is a growing antipathy amongst large sections of the population to the blanket use of synthetic drugs, especially as more and more people are becoming aware of the fact that many diseases are now resistant to the drugs prescribed to combat them. The strong faith in the invincibility of science is waning and this is aggravated by the growing fear of the huge multinational companies in the pharmaceutical industries, which are perceived as being only interested in profit. We have perhaps now seen the bottoming out of the present cycle of interest in healing and increased awareness of the advantages of seeking to bring together the spiritual and the orthodox. More and more doctors faced with little or no improvement in a patient's condition are happy to recommend that he consult a recognised spiritual healer and report back with the results. This should not be seen as an abrogation of the doctor's responsibilities to the patient, but rather an acknowledgement of his willingness to explore all avenues in his search for a cure. In the same way, a responsible healer who is not making progress with a patient will advise him to consult his doctor for tests and further examination. What is now needed is a completely open-minded approach from both sides of the medicinal fence. There should be more contact between doctors and healers, more opportunities to compare notes on the problems of patients and more respect from one side to the other.

We have mentioned earlier the emergence of the New Age movement and the swing away from traditional religions. The actions of some New Agers do tend to alienate vast numbers of ordinary people but it is to be hoped that the idealism of the movement will come to the fore as the Age of Aquarius comes ever nearer. It is also true to say that many of the new evangelical churches which appear to be popular look more kindly on spiritual healing than the more traditional churches have in the past. Many of the traditional churches now have healing services, which are mainly times when prayers are said for sick people known to the congregation. It could perhaps be only a short step to the situation where christian healers conduct healing sessions within a church congregation.

Another factor, which, surprisingly, is persuading people to give more thought to spiritual healing, is the enthusiasm of some members of the royal family for spiritual healing and other complementary therapies. Prince Charles in particular had to endure some ridicule because of his interest in meditation, organic farming and complementary medicine. The ridicule has now evaporated, complementary medicine is attracting much more interest and organically grown foods are now regular items in the supermarkets. The prince has turned his Highgrove farm over completely to organic crops.

What is the future for spiritual healing? One obvious fact is that this ancient therapy will not disappear. The 8,000 healers in the National Federation in Britain will see to that! The present healing cycle certainly appears to be moving upwards and interest is growing due to many of the factors which we have discussed in this book. The greater good of all people would seem to be served better by more obvious co-operation between orthodox medicine and spiritual healing. Even the scientists have to admit that there is much which we still do not know and perhaps more attention should be paid to a healing tradition which has comforted and eased the suffering of mankind for thousands of years.

CONCLUSION

Within the scope of this little book we have considered the place of spiritual healing within the community and also in history. We have looked at some of the influential figures that have impressed themselves on the thinking and the practice of healing. We have seen how the belief in healing has been sustained through the many cycles of popularity and oppression that it has attracted. We have tried to understand more of the place of healing in christianity and other major religions and philosophies. We have tried to show what happens during a healing session, including the experiences felt by the healer and the person receiving the healing.

Complementary therapies often overlap with spiritual healing and there should also be a relationship and co-operation with orthodox medicine.

The history and validity of healing are secure and it is possible that a new upward cycle, just beginning, will take healing to a much higher level of recognition and integration in a much wider alliance in combating the ills of mankind.

FURTHER READING

Arcarti, Kristyna *Gems and Crystals for Beginners* Headway, 1994.

Ashe, Geoffrey *Miracles* Routledge & Kegan Paul Ltd, 1978.

Association for Research & Enlightenment *An Edgar Cayce Health Anthology* ARE Press, Virginia Beach, 1979.

Bach, Edward *Heal Thyself* CW Daniel Co Ltd, 1931.

Balcombe, Betty *As I See It* Piatkus Books, 1996.

Becker, Dr Robert *Cross Currents: the perils of electropollution; the promise of electromedicine* JP Tarcher, 1991.

Becker, Dr Robert *The Body Electric* William Morrow, 1985.

Benor, Dr Daniel *Healing Research; Vols 1-4* Helix, 1993.

Benson, Dr Herbert *Timeless Healing: the power of*

biology and belief Simon & Schuster, 1996.

Benson, Dr Herbert *The Relaxation Response* Avon Books, 1976, 1990.

Brennan, Barbara Ann *Hands of Light: A Guide to Healing Through the Human Energy Field* Bantam, 1988.

Brennan, JH *Occult Reich* Futura Books, 1974.

Bruyere, Rosalyn L *Wheels of Light* Simon & Schuster, 1994.

Buckley, JM *What is the New Age?* Hodder & Stoughton, 1990.

Buckley, Michael *Christian Healing* CTS Publications, 1990.

Buckman, Robert *Magic or Medicine?* Channel Four Books, 1993.

Butterworth, John *Cults and New Faiths* Lion, 1981.

Canfield, Jack & Hansen, Mark Victor *Chicken Soup for the Soul* Health Communications, 1995.

Cayce, Hugh Lynn *Edgar Cayce on Diet and Health* Paperback Library, New York, 1969.

Chapman, George & Stemman, Roy *Surgeon from Another World* The Aquarian Press, 1978.

Chesi, Gert *Faith Healers in the Philippines* Perlinger, 1981.

Chopra, Deepak *Quantum Healing* Bantam Books, 1989.

Collinge, William *Subtle Energies* Warner Books, 1998.

Cornwell, John *Powers of Darkness, Powers of Light* Viking / Penguin Books, 1991.

Cousins, Norman *Anatomy of as Illness* WW Norton, 1979.

Cowens, Deborah *A Gift for Healing* Piatkus Books, 1996.

David, Furlong *The Complete Healer* Piatkus Books, 1995.

De Jonge, Alex *Grigori Rasputin* Collins, 1982.

Dooley, Anne *Every Wall A Door* Abelard Schuman, 1973.

Dossey, Dr Larry *Healing Breakthroughs* Piatkus Books, 1991.

Dossey, Dr Larry Space, *Time and Medicine* Shambala, 1982.

Dossey, Dr Larry *The Healing Power of Words*

Harper, 1993.

Drewery, Eileen *Why Me?* Hodder Headline, 1997.

Eddy, MBG *Science and Health* Boston, 1875.

Edwards, Harry *Thirty Years a Spiritual Healer* Herbert Jenkins, 1968.

Edwards, Harry *The Power of Healing* Tandem, 1967.

Edwards, Harry *A Guide to the Understanding and Practice of Spiritual Healing* Healer Publishing, 1974.

Fulder, Stephen *The Handbook of Alternative & Complementary Medicine* Vermilion, 1997.

Fuller, John *Arigo: Surgeon of the Rusty Knife* Thomas Y Crowell, 1974.

Gerson, Scott *Ayurveda* Element Books, 1993.

Gordon, Stuart *The Paranormal* Headline Books, 1992.

Grills, Joan *Life of Christ* Oxford University Press, 1984.

Haggard, HW *Devils, Drugs and Doctors* Heinemann, n.d.

Harper, Michael *Healings of Jesus* The Jesus Library, 1986.

Harpur, Tom *The Uncommon Touch* McClelland & Stewart, 1995.

Harvey, David *The Power to Heal* Aquarian, 1983.

Hergenhahn, BR *History of Psychology* Wadsworth, 1986.

Hertzberg, Eileen *Healing* Thorsons, 1988.

Hodgkinson, Liz *Spiritual Healing* Piatkus, 1990.

Jackson, Edgar *The Role of Faith in Healing* SCM, 1981.

Jarmon, Dr Robert *Discovering the Soul* ARE Press, 1997.

Keeton, Joe *The Power of the Mind* Robert Hale, 1988.

Kelsey, Morton *Healing and Christianity* SCM, 1973.

Kennet, Francis *Folk Medicine* Marshall Cavendish, 1984.

Kilner, Dr J Walter *The Human Aura* University Books, 1965.

Kroll, Una *In Touch with Healing* BBC Books, 1986.

Large, John Ellis *The Ministry of Healing* Purnell, 1959.

Lawson, David *I See Myself in Perfect Health*

Thorsons, 1994.

Lewis, Dr David C *Healing: fiction, fantasy or fact?* Hodder & Stoughton, 1989.

MacDonald, Allan *A Path Prepared* self-published.

MacNutt, Francis *Healing* Ave Maria Press, 1974.

MacNutt, Francis *The Power to Heal* Ave Maria Press, 1977.

Major, RH *Faiths that Healed* New York, 1940.

Manning, Matthew *In The Minds of Millions* WH Allen, 1977.

Manning, Matthew *No Faith Required* Eikstein Publications, 1995.

Manning, Matthew *The Link* Colin Smythe, 1974.

McGee, Dr Charles T & Chow, Effie Poy Yew *Qigong: Miracle Healing from China* Medi Press, 1996.

McKenna, Paul *The Paranormal World of Paul McKenna* Faber and Faber, 1997.

Maple, Eric *The Dark World of Witches* Pan Books, 1962.

Marnham, Patrick *Lourdes – A Modern Pilgrimage* Heinemann, 1980.

Meel, George *Healers and the Healing Process* Quest

Books, 1977.

Mishlove, Dr Jeffrey *The Roots of Consciousness* Marlow, 1993.

Mitchell, Edgar *Psychic Exploration: a challange for science* Putnam, 1974.

Nash, Wanda *At Ease with Stress* Longman and Todd, 1984.

Nataf, Andre *Dictionary of the Occult* Wordsworth, 1991.

Neame, Alan *Lourdes* Viking / Penguin Books, 1991.

Nolen, Dr William *Healing: A Doctor in Search of a Miracle* Random House, 1974.

O'Neil, Andrew *Charismatic Healing* The Mercier Press, 1988.

Ozaniec, Naomi *Chakras for Beginners* Headway, 1994.

Ozaniec, Naomi *Dowsing for Beginners* Headway, 1994.

Parsons, Stephen *The Challange of Christian Healing* WBC Print, 1986.

Peel, Robert *Spiritual Healing in a Scientific Age* Harper and Row, 1987.

Pellegrino-Estrich, Robert *The Miracle Man* Triad Publishers, 1997.

Pilgrim, Tom *Autobiography of a Spiritualist Healer* Sphere Books, 1982.

Pitts, J *Divine Healing – Fact and Fiction* Arthur James, 1962.

Playfair, Guy Lyon *If This Be Magic* Jonathan Cape, 1985.

Randi, James *The Faith Healers* Prometheus Books, 1987.

Randles, Jenny *The Strange But True Casebook* Piatkus Books, 1995.

Ritchie, Jean *The Secret World of Cults* HarperCollins, 1992.

Rogo, D Scott *Mind Over Matter* The Aquarian Press, 1986.

Rogo, D Scott *Psychic Breakthroughs Today* The Aquarian Press, 1987.

Rose, Louis *Faith Healing* Penguin Books, 1968.

Sanford, Agnes *Healing Gifts of the Spirit* Arthur James, n.d.

Sanford, Agnes *The Healing Light* Arthur James, n.d.

Schul, Bill *The Psychic Frontiers of Medicine* Coronet Books, 1978.

Shaykh, Fadhlalla Haeri *Elements of Sufism* Element Books, 1990.

Sherwood, Keith *The Art of Spiritual Healing* Llewellyn, 1985.

Shiels, WJ *The Church and Healing* Blackwell, 1982.

Shine, Betty *Mind to Mind* Bantam, 1989.

Simonton, Carl & Stephanie *Getting Well Again* Tarcher-St Martin's, 1978.

Singer, Charles *From Magic To Science* Ernest Benn, 1928.

Southwood, Malcolm *The Healing Experience* Piatkus Books, 1994.

Speck, Peter *Loss and Grief in Medicine* Bailliere Tindall, 1978.

Stanway, Dr Andrew *Alternative Medicine – a guide to natural therapies* Macdonald and Jane's, 1979.

Stevens, Anthony *On Jung* Routledge, 1990.

Targ, Russell & Katra Jane *Miracles of the Mind* New World Library, 1998.

Taylor, Allegra *Healing Hands* MacDonald Optima,

1992.

TenDam, Hans *Deep Healing* Tasso Publishing, 1996.

Vitebsky, Piers *The Shaman* DBP, 1995.

Watson, Dr Lyall *Gifts of Unknown Things* Hodder & Stoughton, 1976.

Watson, Dr Lyall *Supernature* Hodder & Stoughton, 1973.

Weil, Dr Andrew *Health and Healing* Houghton Mifflin, 1983.

Werfel, Franz *The Song of Bernadette* Mayflower Books, 1977.

Wills, Pauline *Visualisation for Beginners* Headway, 1995.

Wimber, John *Power Healing* Hodder & Stoughton, 1986.

Woolger, Roger *Other Lives* Other Selves, Bantam Books, 1988.

Worrall, Ambrose and Olga *The Gift of Healing* Rider, 1969.

USEFUL ADDRESSES

UK

Alexander Technique (STAT)

10 London House

266 Fulham Road

London SW10 9EL

Dr Edward Bach Centre

Mount Vernon

Sotwell

Wallingford

Oxon OX10 0PZ

The British Alliance of Healing Associations

Baytrees

47 Beltinge Road

Herne Bay

Kent CT6 6DA

British Touch for Health Association

8 Railey Mews

London NW5 2PA

College of Healing

3 Runnings Park

Croft Bank

West Malvern

Worcs WR14 4BP

Gestalt Centre

64 Warwick Road

St Albans

Herts AL1 4DL

Metamorphic Association

67 Ritherdon Road

London SW17 8QE

National Federation of Spiritual Healers

Old Manor Farm Studio

Church Street

Sunbury on Thames

Surrey TW16 6RF

Natural Health Network

Chardstock House

Chard

Somerset TA20 2TL

Radionic Association

16A North Bar

Banbury

Oxon OX16 0TF

The Shiatsu Society

14 Oakdene Road

Redhill

Surrey RH1 6BT

Silva Foundation

BCM Self Management

London WC1 3XX

Association of Therapeutic Healers

Suite 51

67/69 Chancery Lane

London WC2 1 AF

White Eagle Lodge

New Lands

Brewells Lane

Rake

Liss

Hampshire GU33 7HY

USA

National Spiritualist Association of Churches(NSAC)

PO Box 217

Lily Dale

NY 14752 – 0217

The International Rolf Institue

PO Box 1868

Boulder

Colorado 80306

CANADA

National Federation of Spiritual Healers (Canada)
   Inc

TH 64/331

Military Trail

West Hill

Scarborough

Ontario M5V 3AG

Association of Spiritual Healers of Alberta

40 Edenworld Green N.W.

Calgary

Alberta

T3A 5BA

AUSTRALIA

National Association of ASHA

PO Box 9187

Alice Springs

N T 0871

National Federation of Healers Inc

PO Box 112

Oxenford

Queensland 4210